HOW TO WRITE ABOUT THE MEDIA TODAY

Raúl Damacio Tovares
and
Alla V. Tovares

Writing Today

 GREENWOOD

AN IMPRINT OF ABC-CLIO, LLC
Santa Barbara, California • Denver, Colorado • Oxford, England

Library of Congress Cataloging-in-Publication Data
Tovares, Raúl Damacio, 1952–
    How to write about the media today / Raúl Damacio Tovares and Alla V. Tovares.
      p. cm. — (writing today)
    Includes bibliographical references and index.
    ISBN 978-0-313-37519-4 (hard copy : alk. paper)—ISBN 978-0-313-37520-0
(ebook)
    1. Mass media criticism. 2. Mass media—Authorship. 3. Academic writing—
Vocational guidance. I. Tovares, Alla V. II. Title.
    P96.C76.T68   2010
    808'.066302—dc22   2009048176

ISBN: 978-0-313-37519-4
EISBN: 978-0-313-37520-0

14 13 12 11 10   1 2 3 4 5

This book is also available on the World Wide Web as an eBook.
Visit www.abc-clio.com for details.

Greenwood
An Imprint of ABC-CLIO, LLC

ABC-CLIO, LLC
130 Cremona Drive, P.O. Box 1911
Santa Barbara, California 93116–1911

This book is printed on acid-free paper ∞

Manufactured in the United States of America

CONTENTS

SERIES FOREWORD

Writing is an essential skill. Students need to write well for their coursework. Businesspeople need to express goals and strategies clearly and effectively to staff and clients. Grant writers need to target their proposals to their funding sources. Corporate communications professionals need to convey essential information to shareholders, the media, and other interested parties. There are many different types of writing, and many particular situations in which writing is fundamental to success. The guides in this series help students, professionals, and general readers write effectively for a range of audiences and purposes.

Some books in the series cover topics of wide interest, such as how to design and write Web pages and how to write persuasively. Others look more closely at particular topics, such as how to write about the media. Each book in the series begins with an overview of the types of writing common to a practice or profession. This is followed by a study of the issues and challenges central to that type of writing. Each book then looks at general strategies for successfully addressing those issues, and it presents examples of specific problems and corresponding solutions. Finally, each volume closes with a bibliography of print and electronic resources for further consultation.

Concise and accessible, the books in this series offer a wealth of practical information for anyone who needs to write well. Students at all levels will find the advice presented helpful in writing papers; business professionals will value the practical guidance offered by these handbooks; and anyone who needs to express a complaint, opinion, question, or idea will welcome the methods conveyed in these texts.

CHAPTER 1

Introduction

WHY WE DECIDED TO WRITE THIS BOOK

Since the mid-1800s media technologies have assumed a central role in human interaction. The latest media developments—everything from transnational media corporations to iPods, cell phones, and BlackBerries—have made media technologies and the messages they carry not only a ubiquitous part of modern life, but also an exciting topic for research and writing projects both in and out of academia. With respect to the impact of media technologies on society, one of the most significant developments has been in the way people get news. This is significant because one of the underlying principles of democracy is that citizens have access to information. As newspapers go out of business and more people search for news and information on the Internet, many academics, media practioners, and citizens are asking what impact these changes will have on the democratic process.

While media industries are a powerful force in society, individuals and small groups of people that possess technical skills can also make an impact on modern life. The election of Barack Obama as the 44th president of the United States, especially his use of YouTube, cell phones, and Webcasts to organize and energize his base of supporters, is an example of individuals harnessing the power of new media to make a difference. There are other, less dramatic, stories about using new technologies. Many entrepreneurs have successfully launched for-profit Web sites such as Craigslist. Countless persons have used the new technologies to create successful blogs that allow them to share their thoughts and ideas on a range of issues. At the same time, some media-savvy hustlers are able to steal identities and create problems for individuals by striking a few keys on a computer.

Because of the continuous development of new media and their role in how people create and distribute goods, services, and information—along with increasing enrollments in media studies programs, the spread of opportunities to use the media, and the growth of general interest in the media—we believe there is a need for a book like this one.

WHO SHOULD USE THIS BOOK

How to Write About the Media Today is designed for students at both the high school and college levels, and media practitioners who are facing the challenge of writing about the media. This book covers the various definitions of *media* and guides readers through the process of writing about them. The term *media*, as used in this book, is broadly defined and includes both mass media (print, film, radio, television, and the Internet) as well as other types of media, from drum signals to graffiti. This broad definition of media is in keeping with trends in the numerous media studies departments across the United States and the world and reflects the rapidly changing media landscape. As new media are introduced, older media begin to fade from the media scene, or they take on new functions. For example, on February 2, 2006, the Associated Press reported that Western Union would stop sending telegrams, once the fastest, most convenient way to send a message across long distances. Text messaging, e-mail, relatively inexpensive phone service, and programs such as Skype made telegrams obsolete ("Telegram passes into history," 2006).

Today, iPods and cell phones are the latest media technologies to be widely accepted and used by the public. iPods started as devices on which one could listen to music. When first introduced, iPods were incapable of allowing users to watch movies, videos, and TV shows, take and share pictures, or play games. Few people anticipated watching movies, taking photos, and listening to music on a cell phone, which is the latest reincarnation of an old technology—the telephone. Such unique combinations of the old and the new in media technologies explain why the definition of *media* continues to broaden.

Initially, telephones were a point-to-point means of communication— that is, one person in a particular location called another person in a different location. Today, cell phones are capable of point-to-mass communication. It is dynamic changes such as these, changes that impact society and influence how human beings relate to one another, that make writing about the media an exciting challenge for students and media practitioners.

In addition to the electronic media such as radio, television, film (DVDs), and the Internet, the term *media*, as used in this book, also includes print and speech. This is because, as demonstrated with cell phones and iPods, print and oral forms of communication are increasingly being adapted to new technologies. For example, not so long ago rhetorical studies, which started as the study of persuasion, used to cover oral and print communication. Today, rhetorical studies may include the examination of speeches delivered over YouTube, televised campaign commercials, and presidential debates accessed over Web sites, as well as the investigation of what billboards, television programs, or public spaces communicate (Littlejohn & Foss, 2005, p. 50). The development of media technologies and new definitions of some areas in media studies, along with the impact these changes are having on how people communicate, are only a few examples of why writing about the media offers exciting opportunities to both students and media practitioners.

WHAT THE BOOK COVERS

How to Write About the Media Today covers the process of writing research papers and professional reports, beginning with the selection of a topic and ending with the submission of the final draft. This writing process includes the development and application of research skills. Professional, thoughtful writing about the media demands discipline in how information is found, evaluated, organized, and presented in a well-written research paper or report.

Students enrolled in various communication courses such as journalism, history of communication, mass communication (print, film, radio, television, and the Internet), public speaking, rhetorical studies, public relations, media ethics, organizational communication, and advertising, to name just some of the most obvious areas in media studies, will find this book helpful. This book will also be useful to high school students preparing to do college-level work. Media practitioners, citizen journalists, bloggers, and freelancers can refer to this volume when researching and writing about the media.

Throughout the book, readers will find *Writing Tips* that provide practical information to help them stay on course and reach their goal of a finished paper or report. Along with writing tips, the book also provides its readers with useful time-line suggestions to help research, write, and submit research papers and professional reports on time.

How to Write About the Media Today offers a section on style, basic grammar, and punctuation; sample pages formatted in APA, MLA, and Chicago styles can also be found in the book. Tips for ESL (English as a Second Language) writers, along with a checklist writers can use before submitting their final drafts, are also included. In the age of blogs, e-mails, and text messages it is easy to overlook the importance of grammar and style when trying to convey ideas clearly and gracefully. While this is not a book on grammar, the rules and specific examples in the grammar, style, and punctuation section of the book will help both students and professionals write clearly and effectively.

HOW THE BOOK IS ORGANIZED

How to Write About the Media Today starts with an overview of media studies and moves on to topic selection, research, and writing. It concludes with *Resources for the Future*, an annotated bibliography of helpful resources for media writers. Between the first page and the last, this reference book provides useful information on how to generate a research question, find and evaluate sources, organize information, write a draft, revise a paper or professional report, and, finally, deliver it in a timely manner.

Most media courses, even those that focus on the production aspect of radio or television, may require a term paper or end-of-semester report. Many students are apprehensive about writing such papers. *How to Write About the Media Today* gives students and media practitioners useful information and practical tools—such as writing tips, checklists, and sample research and writing schedules (see Chapter 3)—they can use in their effort to complete a writing assignment. The process of writing about the media is divided into steps that will help students and media practitioners overcome the many challenges encountered when writing about the media.

How to Write About the Media Today may be read sequentially or, because each chapter stands on its own, consulted as needed. For example, a student or media practitioner who has been assigned a topic for a paper or report may skip the section on selecting a topic.

The book can be referred to quickly because of the way it is organized: It promotes an orderly process of writing a media paper, from selecting a topic to formatting a final draft. Subheadings make it easy to locate topics. This organization of the elements of researching and writing papers will help students produce stronger papers that will earn them better grades and boost their self-confidence in their ability to do high-quality work. Furthermore, by becoming better researchers and writers, students will also be investing in their success outside academia, as most professions require and expect their practitioners to be effective writers and communicators. Professionals will want to use this book because it provides them with practical information they can use to write media reports, articles, and other writing assignments from start to finish.

STRUCTURE OF THE BOOK

How to Write About the Media Today is organized into six chapters. Chapter 1, *Introduction*, explains the purpose, scope, and organization of the book. Chapter 2, *What Am I Writing?*, explores the term *media* and what it means to write about the media. The questions "What do researchers write about when they write about the media?" and "How does writing about the media relate to other disciplines?" are also covered.

Chapter 3, *Issues and Challenges*, takes up the concern of writing a successful media paper, including finding reliable sources of information. Locating relevant and reliable information is essential for anyone writing about media or any other topic. In addition to guiding readers through the challenges of searching and evaluating sources, this chapter also offers tools for keeping track of one's progress, such as a research and writing schedule.

Chapter 4 covers strategies for success. Writers learn how to plan ahead, set reasonable goals, use idea-generating exercises, and keep a record of the progress made toward the finished paper or report. Such strategies are designed to ensure that a methodical approach is integrated into the research and writing process. Readers will also find tips on how to develop a good research question, produce a solid thesis statement and support it with evidence, create a helpful outline, and write effective introductions and conclusions.

In Chapter 5, *Problems and Solutions*, readers will find examples of specific problems related to writing about the media, including selecting a media topic, constructing a coherent paper that follows grammar, style, and punctuation conventions, and solutions to those problems. Chapter 5 also addresses difficulties some ESL writers may experience. A brief overview of the formatting styles (APA, MLA, and Chicago), with sample pages in each style, and a checklist for final papers are also included.

Chapter 6, *Resources for the Future*, includes an annotated bibliography that provides quick access to both print and electronic sources useful for media writers.

SUMMARY

This book shows media writers how to generate a topic for a research paper and how to shape that topic into a thesis statement that the paper addresses. It will help those who write about the media to understand what readers—whether professors, editors, supervisors, or general audiences—expect from a paper about media. This book also provides guidelines for researching and evaluating academic books, journal articles, and other sources in order for media writers to access the best information available. Finally, this book shows students and media practitioners how to structure a paper and format it for review by professors, editors, and/or supervisors.

For students, the guidelines provided in this book will help them write strong research papers about various media topics. It will also help them overcome one of the major causes of anxiety among college and high school students: writing research papers. Furthermore, developing good writing and research skills is a way of opening doors to a variety of professional fields. Knowing how to find and use reliable information from respected sources and clearly communicate one's findings in writing is a valuable asset in today's business and professional worlds. In sum, the skills acquired in the course of researching and writing about the media will serve one well in the future, whether or not one remains in the field of media studies.

For media practitioners or writers interested in writing about the media, this book provides useful research and writing tools to produce effective media papers or reports.

ACKNOWLEDGMENTS

We would like to thank those colleagues and friends who have helped us in the production of this book in ways too numerous to list. They will find many of their insightful comments and suggestions reflected in the pages of this book. We are especially grateful to the following reviewers who gave their time and offered valuable suggestions on earlier drafts of this manuscript:

Dianne Forbes-Berthoud, Trinity Washington University
Cynthia Gordon, Syracuse University
Robert Huesca, Trinity University, San Antonio
Brad Mellow, National Communication Association
Michael D. Murray, University of Missouri-St. Louis
Jamey Piland, Trinity Washington University
Diana I. Rios, University of Connecticut
Roger Smitter, National Communication Association
Kent Wilkinson, Texas Tech University

We are also indebted to the Department of English at Howard University for its continuous support of Alla Tovares in her research activities and to the Communication Program at Trinity Washington University for the assistance Raul Tovares received while working on this manuscript. We are grateful to the staff at Greenwood Press for their help in the production of this book. We also benefited from

Julie Wan's comments and suggestions. We would also like to thank our families, especially our parents and siblings, for their support, interest, and understanding of our research and writing endeavors. Last, but not least, we would like to acknowledge our students who have informed our teaching and continue to be a source of professional satisfaction. While we acknowledge the assistance of many people, we recognize that any errors in these pages are ours and ours alone.

REFERENCES

Littlejohn, S. W. & Foss, K. A. (2005). *Theories of human communication* (8th ed.). Belmont, CA: Thomson/Wadsworth.

Telegram Passes into History (2006, February 2). *Associated Press*. http://www.wired.com/science/discoveries/news/2006/02/70147.

CHAPTER 2

What Am I Writing?

This chapter presents a sample of the different topics that can be addressed when writing about the media. Briefly, media papers, essays, and professional reports can examine how media relate to individuals, societies, and culture. The chapter begins with an overview of the different types of media, with a special focus on mass media. It continues with the examination of what the study of media entails and the various topics that can be covered when writing about the media. The chapter concludes with a section that discusses the relationship between writing about the media and writing in other disciplines.

THE MANY MEANINGS OF THE WORD MEDIA

Most people tend to associate the term *media* (plural) with print (books, newspapers, and magazines), film, radio, television, and the Internet. These media, however, are more specifically identified as *mass media*, that is, they have the capacity of reaching a large number of persons. In addition to mass media, there are also smaller media, such as newsletters, low-power radio, and nonprofit local newspapers. A *medium* (singular) is any channel of communication. In recent years it has become acceptable in everyday discourse to use *media* as a singular noun, but in formal writing, when referring to two or more means of communication, it is best to use it as a plural noun (see *Merriam-Webster's Collegiate Dictionary*, 2005, p. 770).

MASS MEDIA

When writing about the mass media one can address a wide range of issues and topics. This is to a large extent due to the size of media companies and their ability to reach large audiences because of the technologies they employ. The ability to send messages to national and international audiences, 24 hours per day, every day of the year, makes mass media content ubiquitous. Never before in history have media been used to instantly send the same message to a large number of people living across the entire world. Today, media companies are national and transnational organizations. As such they are important players in national and international politics and business. This is one aspect of the mass media that makes them worth writing about.

Another aspect of the media that makes them interesting to write about is how the messages they create and distribute influence people's daily activities. For instance, millions of people wake up and turn on a morning television or radio program to hear about events in their community, nation, and the world; they also get the latest weather and/or traffic reports. On the way to work, they might listen to music downloaded the night before from an online source, such as iTunes. At work, many employees check their e-mail messages from individuals and organizations, including news organizations, professional organizations, retailers and social groups. Reports, memos, and calls for meetings or conferences are typically sent via the Internet. In the evening many people watch a TV program, a movie on DVD, or enjoy some other form of entertainment either on a TV set or computer screen. These are all examples of how mass media can influence daily habits. Each of these examples could serve as a topic for a media paper or report.

The mass media can also affect people's lifestyles in other ways. For example, after the release of the film *Sideways* (Payne, 2004), in which the main character expresses his preference for pinot noir wine, sales of this type of wine increased dramatically. One source reported that nationally sales of pinot noir went up 16 percent. In California, the sale of pinot noir increased 33 percent. At the Wild Horse Winery, which is located in the area where most of the movie was shot, pinot noir sales increased by 135 percent (Locke, 2005).

The mass media can also influence behavior with respect to more serious matters, like the importance of medical screenings. In March 2000, Katie Couric, then a co-host on NBC's *Today Show*, underwent a colonoscopy on air as part of a campaign to encourage people to get screened for colon cancer. Researchers (Cram et al., 2003) found that Couric's efforts resulted in a significant increase in the number of persons getting colonoscopies. Also, more women were screened for colon cancer after Couric's campaign than had been reported before.

In addition to influencing individuals, the mass media can also impact large groups of people. For example, the mass media contribute significantly to the formation of a national identity. In many countries mass media were brought under state control for the purpose of producing content that would create or reinforce the idea of belonging to a community beyond the village or town. Whether under state control or independently owned, newspapers, movies, radio programs, and television programs bring news, sounds, and images from distant locations, which causes people to feel that they are connected to a larger, national public (Anderson, 1983; Martín-Barbero, 1993). In newspapers, movies, and radio and television programs, including news reports, stories about people in different cities and states can create or reinforce in the audience a sense of belonging to a national community. Reports about special events such as an inauguration, a patriotic celebration such as a Fourth of July concert, or a presidential news conference can also give viewers a sense of belonging to a community larger than their town or city. Even the reporting of tragic events—such as the 9/11 attacks on the World Trade Center and the Pentagon, and the crash of United Airlines Flight 93 in Somerset County, Pennsylvania—can contribute to a heightened sense of national identity, in this case, of being an American.

The mass media are also considered important to write about because of their relationship to the economy. Media industries are transnational corporations worth billions of dollars and employ millions of people. For example, the largest media company, Time Warner, reportedly earned $34 billion in 2007 just from its media properties. That same year, also just from their media enterprises, the Walt Disney Co. earned $16 billion, and News Corp. earned $14 billion ("100 leading media companies," cited in Campbell, Martin, & Fabos, 2010, p. 426). It is easy to see why the economic health of these companies, whether good or bad, or their sale, can be of interest to readers. Such changes can mean more production or less production, pay raises or job cuts. A sale or merger can also mean that fewer companies are responsible for the production and distribution of news and information, which some media scholars argue may lead to a decrease in the diversity of opinions expressed over media channels (McChesney, 1999). This is an important issue for citizens in a democracy like the United States, which has in its Constitution an amendment allowing the press to serve as a *marketplace of ideas*.

The mass media are also seen as important because they produce cultural products, such as films, television programs, music, video games, and other forms of entertainment and information that can impact people's lifestyles. It has been estimated that by the time someone graduates from high school, he or she has spent almost half of his or her leisure time engaged with media, such as television, radio, newspapers, and magazines. Almost 75 percent of this time is taken up by interaction with a monitor/television (Graber, 2007, p. xxvii). Usually, this is time taken away from other activities, such as studying, playing sports, interacting with family and friends, and attending community meetings.

In sum, the mass media's pervasiveness, their contributions to the construction of a national and personal identity, importance to the economy, role as producers of cultural products, and ability to influence human behavior are some of the reasons why they are considered important and worth writing about. Other media, although not as omnipresent or as influential as mass media, are also important and deserve attention.

OTHER FORMS OF MEDIA

While the mass media may receive more attention from researchers and the general public due to their pervasiveness and impact, smaller media can also play a significant role in communities and the lives of people. A telephone conference call, diary or journal, newsletter, and trade publications are all examples of media. Recall that any channel of communication can be considered a medium. For instance, someone's voice carries information through airwaves that then reach another person's ear. The airwaves cause vibrations in the listener's eardrums, which become signals sent to the person's brain, where the sounds are interpreted as language.

A letter consists of paper and ink and is sent to an addressee, who reads (decodes) the symbols on the paper to understand the information that is being transmitted. These forms of communication—speech and letters—are media, but not mass media, because only a limited number of people who can easily be counted have access to the messages. Consequently, one voice or one letter cannot be expected to have the same impact that a message sent over mass media may have.

There are other forms of communication that can be included under the term *media*, such as drumbeats, whistling, and graffiti. Although most media studies departments do not focus on these forms of media, technically they are media, and in certain classes or for special reports, writing about these forms of media may be appropriate. Centuries before modern means of communication, drums were used by various societies to send signals over long distances (Gardner & Shortelle, 1997). Moreover, Herzog (1964), who studied the Jabo in Liberia, reported that drum signaling can involve different types of drums and thus allow for an elaborate system of signals. In Gomera, in the Canary Islands, people have used a system of whistling, known as *silbo*, to communicate with one another in that area's mountainous terrain (MacLeod, 2004, pp. 156–157). In cities across the world, graffiti, or wall painting, is used to send messages primarily to neighborhood residents (Ferrel, 1995, pp. 277–294).

When people use media they are communicating, that is, sharing information. Media, then, are much more than just the mass media and include other means of communication. What the mass media and smaller media have in common is that in order to understand the messages that are being conveyed, people must have a shared understanding of signs and symbols (see "Study of media and culture").

NEWS MEDIA AND ENTERTAINMENT MEDIA

While the term *media* includes various channels of communication, it is often used in everyday conversation to refer only to news media. When pundits use the terms *the media*, or *the liberal media* or *conservative media*, they are often referring to the news media. While providing news and information is an important function of modern media, the media are much more than just news. For instance, media can also entertain. At the same time, providing news and information is still considered an important role for the media, the mass media especially.

In a democracy, news media are viewed as important because citizens need access to accurate, factual information in order to make informed decisions when voting for one candidate instead of another or when taking a stand on a political issue. A misinformed public may vote for candidates and support policies that can have devastating short-term and long-term consequences (McManus, 1994, p. 4). This is why citizens depend on news producers to deliver information that is unbiased and free of errors. Information delivered as news is expected to be true and not distorted, biased, or in any way misleading. The news can be entertaining, but its value rests on an understanding between the producers of news and the consumers of news that it is factual, complete, and informative. The importance of providing accurate information to citizens in a democracy is the primary reason why the news media gets so much attention from those who analyze the media.

Media writers who cover the news media tend to focus on the news media's role in society. The news media's coverage of the events leading up to the war in Iraq, especially their failure to report fairly and accurately on the lack of intelligence regarding that country's weapons of mass destruction, the anticipated positive reaction of the Iraqis to the presence of U.S. military, the collapse of the world financial system, and the home mortgage crisis in the United States, among a host of other issues, have all raised questions about the news media's role as a source of unbiased and factual information. Many news media observers agree that the news media have failed in their role to keep readers abreast of what is actually happening in politics and the economy, and instead have become cheerleaders for government policies and Wall Street schemes (Starkman, 2009, pp. 24–30).

The failure of the mainstream media to provide accurate and balanced information about Iraq's lack of weapons of mass destruction and reckless investment practices on Wall Street has occurred at the same time that traditional news media are losing readers, listeners, and viewers. The economic failure of many news media and the failure of many mainstream U.S. news media to accurately inform the public have led some to call for new business models for news production that are not advertiser-based (see Picard, Stearns, & Aaron, n. d.). Such proposals provide many research opportunities for media writers covering the issue of the news media and their role in society.

Unlike news, entertainment media programs, such as sitcoms, crime dramas, news parodies, late-night talk shows, and music, are expected to deliver fictional or distorted material. The material may be based on facts ("ripped from the headlines"), but it need not, nor is it expected to, stick to the facts. Such entertainment media can be entertaining without necessarily informing the audience. Many songs, television programs, magazine columns, and other forms of media are produced solely to entertain. In fact, some would argue that one of the purposes of such programming is to distract the audience from the serious issues that are often delivered via the news media (Postman, 1985).

Entertainment via the media comes in many forms. A situation comedy or police drama on television is a form of entertainment. So is a sporting event. Most people would agree that news about sports is usually more entertainment than it is news. A soccer player making a field goal may be important to fans of the team, but this achievement is not likely to make much of a difference in national or world politics. This is not to say that entertainment is not important. Radio and television programs, music, films, and the newer forms of entertainment, such as YouTube, can have a big impact on people's lives. Sometimes, entertainment programs can be just as, if not more, informative as news programs because under the guise of entertainment they can tackle important sociopolitical issues and raise awareness about the issues they present. A good example is *The Daily Show with Jon Stewart*. Stewart's parody of television news serves to expose not only the shortcomings and hypocrisy of politicians and business leaders, but of the entire news business as well. In addition, in order to fully understand the humor in programs like *The Daily Show with Jon Stewart*, one needs to stay abreast of the reports aired on more "serious" newscasts. Many of the jokes on *The Daily Show* will make little sense without background knowledge about current events. The role of parody in political discourse, which is closely related to the topics of freedom of speech and the press, can provide media writers with a number of topics for papers and reports.

NEW MEDIA TECHNOLOGIES AND NEWS AND ENTERTAINMENT

The role of new media technologies and their impact on politics and culture is another topic that receives attention from media writers. Relatively new media technologies, such as hand-held video recorders, YouTube, iPods, and cell phones, are influencing news and entertainment. In 1991, amateur photographer George Holliday recorded the beating of Rodney King, who was stopped for speeding by members of the Los Angeles Police Department and beaten with nightsticks. News programs across the United States and the world played Holliday's recordings. The images of the beating, recorded with inexpensive, small, portable equipment, made a deep and lasting effect on many viewers (Gilmore, 1993, pp. 28–29).

Radio programs, such as the Don Imus show (CBS's *Imus in the Morning*) on April 7, 2007, made an impact on people's lives when the host of the program used derogatory terms when referring to the Rutgers University women's basketball team (http://nbcsports. msnbc.com/id/17982146/ and http://www.cbsnews.com/stories/2007/ 04/12/national/main2675273.shtml). Not only were the women on the Rutgers basketball team offended, but so were many other people across the country. Imus's comments were posted on YouTube and watched by millions of persons who had not heard the statements on Imus's program. The statements' presence on YouTube contributed significantly to the growing protests over Imus's remarks and calls for his dismissal. A week later, CBS fired Imus.

The year before Imus made his racist remarks, S. R. Sidarth was following the senatorial campaign of George Allen and recording the U.S. senator's speeches on a handheld video camera. Allen was leading his opponent, Jim Webb, by as much as 20 percentage points in some polls. Many political observers believed that Allen's next step after the senate election would be a run for the White House. A video recording of Allen at a political rally in Breaks Interstate Park, Virginia, in August 2006, ended those plans.

The Allen campaign was aware that Sidarth, a member of the Indian community in Virginia, supported Jim Webb. Sidarth was "tracking" Allen's speaking tour through the southern part of the state. Tracking in this context means following a candidate and videotaping his or her speeches and conversations with supporters in the hopes of capturing the candidate making a sexist remark, racist comment, or some other type of offensive or embarrassing statement.

At the Breaks rally, Allen referred to Sidarth as "macaca" and said, "Welcome to America and the real world of Virginia." The term *macaca* refers to a genus of Asian monkeys, but is also sometimes used as a racial slur. Sidarth had captured Allen's remarks on video, which he gave to the Webb campaign, which posted the clip on YouTube (Jordan, 2008).

Allen quickly issued an apology for the remark. He also met with leaders of the Indian community in an attempt to put the incident behind him. However, YouTube gave the Breaks rally incident a life of its own. One source claimed that the Allen video became one of the most visited sites on YouTube. A few weeks after the Allen video was posted on YouTube, his challenger, Jim Webb, was elected U.S. senator from Virginia. According to Sidarth, "If I had been there and not had a camera with me, absolutely, no one would have believed my side of the story" (Jordan, 2008, p. 80).

Even comedians, who are usually given more leeway than politicians when it comes to topics such as race and gender, can be negatively affected by new media technologies. Michael Richards, while performing at the Laugh Factory on November 17, 2006, made racist remarks that were caught on cell phone video and posted on YouTube. The following year, Richards announced his retirement as a stand-up comic (McDermid, 2007). While many comedians are known for jokes that cross lines of decency and racial boundaries, the fact that Richards's comments were recorded on cell phones and posted on the Internet gave others who were not at his performance a chance to listen to and evaluate the material. Richards is seen on the YouTube video making his remarks and taunting the hecklers even as they are leaving the club. With Richards, as with Allen, the YouTube postings made the material permanent rather than a fleeting moment.

New portable media and easy-to-use computer programs are facilitating the creation of an army of citizen journalists. Cameras that fit in the palm of one's hand and Weblogs, or blogs (online journals that can be shared with the world), make it easy to set up shop as a reporter. This phenomenon raises important questions for media writers: Are these citizen journalists, many of whom have no training in journalism, prepared to inform their communities about people, events, and government policies? What qualifies them to do so in a fair and accurate manner? If they are qualified, what does this say about the training of professional journalists? If they are not qualified, should citizen journalists be trained to find, research, and report news, and how should they be educated about the role of news and information in society? If they receive the same training as mainstream journalists, will this training and education only lead to the same news and information the news media are producing today? These are not only major issues that are currently being discussed in media classes and in newsrooms but also viable topics for media papers or reports.

All of the examples discussed above show how new media technologies are having an impact on people's everyday lives. It's not only "news and information" transmitted by the media that can make a difference in an individual's life and in society. How and what messages these new media communicate and their relevance to everyday life are topics that can be covered when writing about the media.

While the line between the news media and entertainment media may not always be clear, students and media practitioners who write about the news media or entertainment media are expected to report their findings accurately and objectively. Media papers and reports should not be presented in the form of blogs or infotainment, or even journalistic writing. Instead, media papers and reports should strive to meet the highest standards of academic writing (see Chapter 5 for more information about the academic style of writing).

MEDIA AND EVERYDAY LIFE

Because media are so pervasive, almost everything human beings do today is in some way linked to media. For example, friends and family members, as well as business associates and clients, can be reached by phone. Phones are also used to send and receive text messages, photographs, and short videos (words, still images, and moving images). For many individuals in industrialized nations, communicating via e-mails or text messages has become a part of their daily routine. It has also come to be expected that persons on vacation will send digital photos of their destination(s) to family and friends back home. Such widespread media presence in people's daily lives is made possible by changes in how media products are distributed, including their format. Furthermore, advances in technology have led to the merger of what used to be distinct media.

Movies, which not too long ago could only be seen on theater screens, have become more accessible. Movies can now also be seen on iPods, cell phones, computers, screens in front of video projectors, and TV sets. Newspapers can be read in either hardcopy or online. There are also a growing number of e-books and audiobooks. Radio programs are shared on iPods or computer screens or "burned" on CDs. Music is downloaded from on-line music stores. These developments are the result of technological innovations, such as the digitization of media signals.

Digitization is the "translation" of messages from their original form, such as a page with print, a film, or painting, into ones and zeros, the basis for the language of computers. This translation has become the standard format for sending and receiving information. The move from analog signals to digital signals has led to what is known as *media convergence*. Media that were once distinct—film and radio signals for example—have merged to create and distribute new products. Today a film, which used to exist as images on narrow, thin sheets of light-sensitive plastic hundreds of feet long, can be translated into ones and zeros that can either be recorded on a DVD or transmitted via satellite to remote areas and viewed on computer screens.

In addition to the convergence of media formats, there is also the convergence of media industries. For example, a newspaper company may own a television station. A television network might own a film studio. A music company may own a billboard company. These mergers and acquisitions are believed to streamline production. For example, a television reporter who works for a station that also owns a newspaper may produce a story for the evening broadcast and use the same information to write a story for the newspaper's Web site.

The trend toward convergence represents a shift in thinking among media executives. In the early days of radio and television, Hollywood jealously guarded its business until it realized it was only shooting itself in the foot. For example, in the early days of radio, Hollywood studio chiefs prohibited their actors from making radio appearances. It was not until it became obvious that a radio appearance by an actor promoted the actor's movies that the policy was changed (Sklar, 1994, p. 277). Another manifestation of the early exclusionary policies of Hollywood was its relationship with television. In the early days of television, Jack Warner of Warner Brothers Studios did not allow television sets to appear in movies made by his studio. The belief was that if television sets did not appear in movies, the new medium would eventually die out (Barnouw, 1990, p. 193). Ironically, today the majority of television programs are produced in Hollywood. In the 1930s, soon after radio stations began using newspapers to assemble news reports, newspaper publishers attempted to copyright the facts in their stories and charge radio stations for using them on air (Campbell, Martin, & Fabos, 2010, p. 258). Today, newspaper stories are often discussed on radio programs, and on television programs news commentators will often hold up a copy of a newspaper and then proceed to discuss a story printed on one of its pages. Such prominence can increase the sale of newspapers.

The convergence of media and media industries is an important topic for media writers because these mergers change how the media operate in society and in turn affect how people work and relax. As a result of media convergence, more people than ever before interact with media at home and at work. With new video technology, viewers at home can not only enjoy their favorite movies, they can also add their own commentary, a feature previously reserved for the creators of movies. Today, many employees—some estimate the number to be from 12 to 14 million—have the option of telecommuting to work from their home at least once a week (Tahmincioglu, 2007). At school, homework assignments and class lectures can be delivered via the Internet using online educational programs. Entire college courses of study can be accessed from home. In fact, today, many students receive degrees without ever setting foot on a college campus. Some virtual communities are, to some extent, replacing, or at least changing, actual communities. For example, video conferencing and chat rooms have made it possible for many organizations and committees that previously met in offices, conference rooms, or social halls to hold meetings online in a virtual conference room. In some cases new media are creating new communities. Online clubs and organizations have sprung up to meet a need, provide a service, or simply to offer friendship. Of course, the same media that encourage persons to seek like-minded folks for support and friendship have also made it possible for others, cyber predators, to take advantage of people by pretending to be someone they are not.

In some cases, media make us feel safer and facilitate everyday life. Apartment buildings, university campuses, banks, office building lobbies, and stores are equipped with video surveillance cameras. Bank computers process transactions when money is withdrawn or transferred using an ATM machine and let us know how much money we can spend, or how much we have overspent. Scanning machines allow shoppers to self-checkout at stores and to check in at the airport without ever interacting with a human being. Announcements about sales, discounts, and free gifts, as well as bank statements and travel itineraries, are delivered by e-mail. So too are office memos, party invitations, and the daily lunch specials at our favorite deli. While many appreciate the convenience afforded by new media, others are concerned about the privacy issues raised by such convenience. For example, businesses often track a customer's purchases without the customer's knowledge and sell that information to interested parties.

While the extent to which media touch daily life is of concern to many observers of media, it is good news for those who write about the media because it means that a variety of social phenomena can be researched and written about from a media angle. After all, what aspect of our lives is not affected either directly or indirectly by media? Media and their relationship to individuals, society, and culture provide numerous possibilities for research papers, essays, and reports.

THE STUDY OF MEDIA

The study of media is not well defined (Littlejohn & Foss, 2005, p. 275) or confined to one academic department of a college or university. One reason for this is that, as pointed out above, the media themselves are constantly changing and evolving. For example, the Internet, up until a few decades ago, was a medium of communication designed for military purposes. It was only after the National Science Foundation set up a communications network in the early 1980s that academics and college students started using e-mail and File Transfer Protocols that the Internet began to develop into a mass medium (Campbell, et al., 2010, pp. 46–47).

As the media develop and touch the lives of more and more people, an increasing number of academics become interested in them. These researchers bring their own perspectives to the study of media. Some sociologists and social psychologists, for example, point out that the study of media is nothing more than the examination of media from a sociological or social-psychological perspective. Such a view is referred to as a society-centric approach to the study of media. Other scholars argue that media are inherently different and that, because of their influence on society and individuals, the study of media deserves its own approach, a media-centric approach (see McQuail, 1994, p. 3).

As noted earlier, the study of media is constantly changing and developing as are media themselves. Some media develop into mass media, while others fade away. For example, initially newspapers were simply media, and not mass media. This is because when newspapers were first published, both in Europe and the American Colonies, most of the population was illiterate, so only a small number of the educated elite read newspapers. Accordingly, the small number of potential readers made early newspapers expensive. In the American Colonies, the annual subscription to a newspaper was about the same as the weekly wage of the average worker; moreover, the subscription had to be paid in full at the time it was ordered.[1] Newspapers became affordable to large numbers of people during the industrial revolution when literacy rates began to rise, and the mass production of newspapers, coupled with advertising that subsidized their production, led to a drop in their cost. Thus, newspapers became a mass medium several centuries after Gutenberg designed his first printing press in the mid-1400s (McQuail, 2004, p. 2).

In contrast to newspapers, other forms of technology or equipment for transmitting messages, such as record players, have almost disappeared. At one time, roughly the 1960s and 1970s, having a stereo system that included a turntable, amplifier, and speakers was very popular. Records, or LPs (long play), were played on the stereo system and provided music for individuals, parties, and other types of special events. Today, most people prefer to program their iPods and channel digital music through a speaker system or headphones. It is important to keep in mind that while the technology has changed, the concept, playing back and enjoying recorded music, has remained the same. Often someone will make the statement that the media, especially new media, have "changed everything." This is, of course, a gross exaggeration. It is important not to lose sight of the links between the old and new technologies. E-mail, for instance, is an electronic version of letters sent via the postal system. Likewise, reading newspapers online is not unlike reading newspapers in hard copy. The media certainly change many things, but they do not change everything. However, this tension between the old and new media offers exciting research opportunities.

On college campuses, the study of media usually covers the mass media (listed above) and related topics, such as, but not limited to, the impact of media on individuals, society, and culture. A sampling of the topics culled from the curricula of some university media studies departments/programs/centers across the United States yields the following list, in no particular order:

Media Theory
Introduction to Media Studies
Video Field Production
Journalism
Documentary Films
History of Media
New Latin American Cinema
Audio Production
Media and the First Amendment
Media Ethics
International Media
Media Law
Media and Civil Society
Politics and Media
Role of Media in Society
Popular Culture
New Media Technologies
African Films
Asian Films
Latino Media in the U.S.
Queer/Lesbian/Transgender Film Studies
Media and Cultural Diversity
Minority Representation in American Media
Introduction to Mass Communication
Media and Violence
Media and Public Health
Audience Research
Media Effects
Media and Education
Media Industries

Obviously, the study of media covers a wide area. One of the reasons for such a broad range of topics is that in some colleges and universities the study of media is often associated with different fields, such as communication studies, journalism, and film studies. Many universities have communication departments that include media studies as part of the curriculum. Still others separate schools of journalism from communication departments or communication programs. The University of Missouri-Columbia, for example, has a School of Journalism and a Communication Department. The Communication Department includes interpersonal communication, mass communication, organizational communication and political communication (http://www.missouri.edu/academics/departments.php). The University of Iowa also has a separate School of Journalism and Mass Communication and a Communication Studies Department. In addition, it also has a Department of Cinema and Comparative Literature (http://www.uiowa.edu/~ccl/). Communication studies departments typically cover the mass media as well as areas such as rhetorical studies, interpersonal communication, small group communication, and organizational communication.

Students and media practitioners who write about the media should be aware of the difference between the study of media, or media studies, and a branch of media studies that developed from cultural studies. Cultural media studies, a critical approach to the study of the mass media, traces its origins back to the work of Williams (1960), Hoggart (1957), and Thompson (1963). The purpose of Cultural Studies, was summed up by Hall (1990) as a way of "enabl(ing) people to understand what [was] going on, and especially to provide ways of thinking, strategies for survival, and resources for resistance" (cited in Grossberg, Nelson, & Treichler, 1992, p. 2). Cultural media studies questions the role of media institutions, their purpose, and the intentions of their corporate owners. It views the media as a site of negotiation between the ideas of the elite and those of the consumers of media products. It also sees media as important industries that can influence the production of culture, while social scientific approaches tend to see the role of the media in society as more neutral, akin to reflectors of culture rather than active participants in the creation of culture. Media studies departments can include researchers who work from both a social scientific perspective and researchers who work from a Cultural Studies perspective (see Downing, 2004, for an overview of the field of media studies and Grossberg, Nelson, & Treichler, 1992, for an overview of Cultural Studies, esp. pp. 1–22).

ORIGINS OF THE STUDY OF MASS MEDIA

Scholarly interest in the mass media started around the very late 1800s to the early 1900s, when there was concern with the growing popularity of newspapers, film, radio, and the phonograph. Political, religious, and community leaders worried about the effects of these new media on individuals and societies. More specifically, their worries were centered on the perceived harmful effects these media might have on the working and middle classes and the young. The fear was that these new media would lead many citizens, especially younger ones, to replace knowledge derived from formal learning, such as appreciation for the classic forms of art, theater, and music, with what they were learning from more popular forms of entertainment, such as the tabloids, vaudeville, popular music, and movies. Much of the concern centered on the effect of these media on the sexual behavior of the young. Also, because some media (known as "muckraking" newspapers and magazines) were exposing corruption in government and industry and portraying community leaders in a less-than-flattering light, there was fear among the elite that such information would lead to a loss of respect for not only the community's political, religious, and civic leaders, but for traditional values as well. It was primarily for these reasons that scholars from various fields, such as psychology, sociology, and philosophy, became interested in these new media (see McQuail, 2004, pp. 1–17 for a brief history of the development of media studies). For example, in 1916, Hugo Münsterberg, a psychologist, published *The Photoplay: A Psychological Study* about the then new medium of film. His work is considered the first scholarly examination of film and its impact on individuals. At the time, Münsterberg was head of what was called the Philosophical Department at Harvard University (see Griffith, 1970, p. vii).

Although cheap, mass produced, sensationalistic newspapers, known as "Penny Papers," can be traced back to the 1830s, a rapid increase in newspaper production and distribution roughly between 1890 and 1920—due to funding of public education, a growing literate immigrant community, and the growth of advertising—raised concerns about the effects that newspapers were having on readers. This was a time when sensationalistic headlines and lurid stories, a style of coverage known as "Yellow Journalism," were shamelessly used to sell newspapers. This was also the time when the immigrant press, much of it printed in languages other than English, had a strong presence. Many civic leaders worried that foreign language papers reinforced old-world languages, ideas, and values at the expense of the English language and "American" values and ideas. Sociologist Robert Park of the University of Chicago published *The Immigrant Press and its Control* (1922). In contrast to popular fears and beliefs about the immigrant press, he reported that, rather than promoting separatism, the immigrant press helped newly arrived residents learn about the United States and provided them with information that allowed them to adapt to the social and political ways of the new country. Later, between 1929 and 1932, the Payne Study and Experimental Fund would provide a grant to the Motion Picture Research Council to investigate the effects of movies on children (Sklar, 1994, p. 135). In 1935, Gordon Allport and Hadley Cantril published their study, *The Psychology of Radio*. One of the reasons for the study was concern about radio as a form of social control (1986, p. vii). Thus, the first studies of mass media were the result of concerns about social issues such as respect for authority, moral standards, immigration, and assimilation. The concerns of political, civic, and religious leaders and the work of researchers in the early part of the twentieth century were the basis for today's multidisciplinary study of media. With respect to writing about the media, one result of the number of concerns about media and the variety of perspectives used to study them is a plethora of topics that media writers can explore. Students and media practitioners do not have the problem of finding a topic, but of deciding on one.

STUDY OF MEDIA AND CULTURE

Another reason the study of media offers such a wide array of possibilities for research is that at its core is the investigation of how symbol systems, such as language, writing, film, paintings, and music, are created and transmitted, and how these symbol systems give meaning to our lives (Masterman, 1994, p. 20; Mead, 1934; Peirce, 1991; Saussure, 1959). To be more precise, the study of media is the study of how signs and symbols are used to transmit cultural values.

The media, like all systems of communication, were created by humans. This is why human communication is an artifact. Moreover, the symbols and signs of human communication are arbitrary. For example, the sounds and letters of a language are not inherently connected to meaning. While it is true that humans possess a voice box, which allows them to produce sounds, and have ears through which they hear, the meaning given to the sounds is agreed upon, or socially constructed (Berger & Luckmann, 1989). The same principle of arbitrariness of meaning applies to visual (written and sign language, photography, film) and tactile (Braille) forms of communication. For example, the letters D–O–G are understood to mean a four-legged creature that barks, usually bigger than a cat but smaller than a horse. When people read the word *dog* or hear it spoken, they imagine the animal that has a tail, barks, and, in Western society at least, often lives in people's homes. But if the Spanish word *perro* or the Russian word *sobaka* is used in front of listeners who neither speak nor understand Spanish or Russian, their reaction will be a blank stare. Put differently, nothing in the words *perro* or *sobaka* connects them to their meaning. This is how we can determine that there is no direct, natural correlation between the sound and spelling of a word and its meaning. It should be noted that each language has a limited set of words, onomatopoetic words, in which the form has a somewhat non-arbitrary relation to the meaning. However, even then, a Spanish-speaking person would hear a dog's barking as "wow-wow," while for a Russian speaker it would be "gav-gav." Thus, in general, the meaning ascribed to words had to be agreed upon by a community. Language, whether spoken or written, visual or auditory, is essential for human beings and is, therefore, a part of culture. When people study communication, they are also studying culture (Carey, 1992; Downing & O'Connor, 1995, pp. 3–22).

Words and their meanings are part of culture and passed on to other members of the community. When communicating, human beings are recreating their culture. It is in this sense that the study of media focuses on life as seen through human interaction. In the process of communicating with one another, either face-to-face or through the mass media, human beings both re-create and reinforce their culture.

CULTURE

Culture is a difficult concept to define (Bouchard, 2006; Eagleton, 2000; Williams, 1981). Scholars have debated the definition of culture for thousands of years. Some people still hold on to the idea of "culture" as artistic forms like poetry, opera, ballet, classical music, and great literature. These art forms are sometimes labeled "high culture." Some people who write about culture tend to categorize different forms of expression as either high culture or mass culture (Arnold, 1911; MacDonald, 1965; and see Levine, 1990, for an historical account of how culture in the U.S. came to be classified as "low," "middle," and "high."). Today most scholars think of culture in broader terms (Carey, 1992; Rosaldo, 1989, p. 26; Williams, 1960). As Geertz (1973) writes, the concept of culture "denotes an historically transmitted pattern of meanings embodied in symbols, a system of inherited conceptions expressed in symbolic forms by means of which men communicate, perpetuate, and develop their knowledge about and attitudes toward life" (p. 89). Most media scholars understand culture as a broad concept of how we live our daily lives and media as channels of communication that carry messages and cultural values. The mass media are channels that transmit cultural values on a large scale.

Part of any discussion of culture will inevitably include the topic of ideology. Like culture, ideology is also difficult to define (Eagleton, 1991; Williams, 1960). In general, however, ideology is understood as the ideas, values, and beliefs that drive people's actions. For many media researchers, the topics of media, culture, ideology, and human action are intertwined. For example, Fiske (1989) views culture as "the constant process of producing meanings of and from our social experience" (p. 1). Fiske goes on to explain that these meanings, in turn, produce a social identity. Social identity is tied to ideology. Human beings develop a sense of who they are—that is, their identity—by accepting at least some of the prevailing ideas, values, and beliefs of their community. For instance, someone who identifies as an American tends to believe in freedom, democracy, and individual initiative.

In U.S. culture, individual initiative is highly valued. Persons are expected to be independent, take care of themselves, and be self-reliant. This expectation rests on the belief that individual initiative is the basis for motivating members of society to work hard, which in turn contributes to the common good. Individuals who show initiative and create businesses provide jobs for members of the community; they contribute to the tax base and may even donate part of their company's profits to charitable organizations. According to the logic of U.S. mainstream ideology, everyone benefits from individual initiative. Therefore, it is not surprising that many films, television programs, including news programs, and magazine articles stress the importance of individual initiative. In this way, the news and entertainment media support the value placed on individual initiative and contribute to the maintenance of this cultural belief or ideology.

In line with this ideology, without the guarantee of help from government agencies, individuals are supposed to be even more motivated to succeed. Economic opportunities are created to motivate persons to take a chance, work hard, and succeed. Although there is always the possibility of failure, the rewards of success are a great motivator.

Yet the news media have also reported that the U.S. government bailed out banks and investment firms when they made mistakes, gambled, and lost. Such contradictions and their negotiation are the meeting point where ideology is worked out, and in the process, culture is created and re-created (see Hall, Clarke, Critcher, Jefferson, &

Roberts, 1978). How the media, especially the news media, make sense of such events is another area of media studies that can provide many topics for papers and reports.

In addition to knowing what they can write about, it is also important for media writers to understand that ultimately the purpose of writing about the media is to promote media literacy. Media literacy provides readers with the tools that allow them to go beyond the words, sounds, and images that make up media messages and raise questions about media institutions and their owners as well as the content that is produced. Media literacy allows consumers of media content to understand their relationship to media and learn how to detect bias due to technology, ownership patterns, and the economic and political forces that shape production (see Masterman, 1994; Inglis, 1990, for more about media literacy).

WRITING ABOUT THE MEDIA AND WRITING IN OTHER DISCIPLINES

Writing about the media shares some characteristics with writing in other fields, such as art, history, philosophy, psychology, and sociology, to name just a few. In fact, as mentioned above, the study of media developed from these other fields (Czitrom, 1982; McQuail, 1994). The study of media is a crossroads where the media interests of researchers from a variety of fields intersect. It is at this crossroads that diverse areas of research inform and enrich one another. Media scholars borrow from other fields of inquiry, and many scholars from various fields find themselves researching and writing about the media. Two of the first researchers to investigate how the media influence people and societies, Paul Lazarsfeld and Harold Lasswell, were sociologists. More recently, sociologist Michael Schudson (1978) and historian Erik Barnouw (1990) have written about the history of media. Noam Chomsky, a linguist, and Edward Herman, an economist, have written about the role of the news media in society (1988). Other scholars, such as Albert Bandura (1986), L. Rowell Huesmann and Leonard Eron (1986), relying mainly on theories of psychology, have studied and reported on the effects of television violence. Using sociological theories, some media scholars study how media technologies influence the organization of society. Many media scholars draw on resources from other fields besides psychology and sociology. For example, much of film criticism is rooted in literary studies as well as the philosophy of art, especially as it relates to painting and photography. Drama/theater studies also influence film criticism. Studies of violence on television and film often draw on the fields of psychology and sociology. These different academic approaches and theoretical perspectives are two of the reasons that make the study of media an exciting area of research.

Because there is so much overlap between the study of media and other academic fields, writing about the media shares many characteristics with, writing in these other fields. For example, writing about the history of film brings together both film studies and history. One of the golden rules of historians is to go to original documents. Film historians follow the same rule. The same can be said about economists who write about some aspect of the mass media. An essay on the economics of television might be descriptive or rely heavily on statistics and incorporate business formulas. An essay that analyzes the lyrics of a recently released song may rely on methods similar to those used to analyze poems.

Similar to research in the social sciences, media research can move from a general topic to specific examples and vice versa. For example, when studying the negative effects of media, a general topic, researchers often write about specific incidents such as the one associated with the Disney movie *The Program* (Ward, 1993). In the original version of that film, college football players are seen lying down in the middle of a highway late at night to prove their courage. After the movie was released, several incidents across the country were reported in which high school students lay down in the middle of busy highways late at night. Some of these incidents resulted in tragedy. One student was killed, while others were seriously injured after they were run over by cars ("Disney Plans to Omit Film Scene . . .," *New York Times*, October 20, 1993, p. A21; see also Wines, 1993). A media essay on the effects of films on adolescents may start with reports about teenagers who imitate dangerous behavior—that is, it will move from a specific case to the general trend. In this case, the general trend was that of the millions who watched *The Program*, an overwhelming number did not lie down in the middle of a busy highway. To contextualize a paper on the topic of the effects of the film *The Program*, a writer should dedicate one section of the paper to a review of the major theories and important studies that have examined media effects. Such a review should include, for example, the once-popular belief that media are all-powerful and have a direct and intense effect on people, often referred to as the *hypodermic needle model* of the mass media. The name of this model of mass communication, never a formal academic theory, derived from the belief that the media had the power to inject ideas into people's minds. The 1938 radio broadcast of H. G. Welles's *War of the Worlds*, produced and written by Orson Welles, and the use of film and radio by the Nazi government in Germany in the 1930s and 1940s helped promote the idea that the mass media could be used to control people's thoughts and behavior. Although Welles aired a disclaimer at the start of the program that what the audience was about to hear was a radio play, persons who tuned in late believed that they were hearing a live broadcast of a Martian invasion of Earth. The broadcast caused panic among many listeners (Cantril, 2005). Some scholars also interpreted the Nazi Party's use of radio and film in the 1930s and 1940s as evidence of the power of these forms of mass communication to manipulate and control the population of a nation. There is no denying that the Nazis took over German mass media once they were in power (see Pratkanis & Aronson, 2000, p. 319). Today there is greater appreciation for the context in which media messages are produced and distributed. There is also a greater appreciation for the diversity of ways that audience members interpret, or decode, media messages.

Another similarity between the study of media and other academic fields is that they all cover a vast array of topics—from the economics of production to the visual arts. Under the media umbrella are topics that deal with virtually all forms of communication. The study of media, then, may include an examination of the earliest clay tablets used in Mesopotamia to record information (around 4000 B.C.E.) as well as the latest technological developments used for mass communication, like cell phones and Internet-based social-networking sites like Twitter. Such a span of time makes it possible to write about the media that were used in different historical periods.

SUMMARY

Since the early days of the Industrial Revolution, when steam power was harnessed to run printing presses in the 1830s, people have increasingly depended on the mass media for information and entertainment. In fact, today it is impossible to understand how individuals can live from day to day without asking questions about the media and their relationship to society. The media—whether the airwaves that carry the sound of human voices, the light waves that carry visual information, or the satellite dishes and wires that send and receive electronic signals—affect how people see themselves and the world around them. This is why it can be said that when writing research papers and reports about the media, writers are engaged in a conversation to understand how media shapes everyday life. Through well-researched essays, media writers can help readers understand the role of media in their daily lives.

The subject of media offers a large number of possibilities for research papers, essays, and reports. Media topics can be classified in different ways. While mass media are often what people have in mind when they are discussing "the media," other forms of media also present an array of topics for research papers, essays, and reports. In sum, students and professionals have numerous options to choose from in terms of topics or subjects for research. Almost any social or human phenomenon can be studied from a media perspective. The following chapters provide a more detailed approach to writing about the media.

NOTE

1. We would like to thank Jim N. Green of the Library Company of Philadelphia for this information regarding the price of newspapers during the Colonial Period.

REFERENCES

Allport, G. & Cantril, H. (1986). *The psychology of radio*. Salem, NH: Ayer Company. (Original work published 1935).

Anderson, B. (1983). *Imagined communities: Reflections on the origin and spread of nationalism*. London: Verso.

Arnold, M. (1911). *Culture & anarchy: An essay in political and social criticism*. New York: Macmillan and Co.

Bandura, A. (1986). *Social foundations of thought and action: A social cognitive*. Englewood Cliffs, NJ: Prentice Hall.

Barnouw, E. (1990). *Tube of plenty: The evolution of American television*. New York: Oxford University Press.

Berger, P. & Luckmann, T. (1989). *The social construction of reality: A treatise in the sociology of knowledge*. New York: Anchor Books.

Bouchard, M. (2006). Culture, characteristics of. In *Encyclopedia of anthropology*. Sage Publications. Retrieved June 29, 2009, from http.www.sage-reference.com/anthropology/article_n233.html.

Campbell, R., Martin, C. R., & Fabos, B. (2010). *Media & culture: An introduction to mass communication*. Boston: Bedford/St. Martins.

Cantril, H. (2005). *The invasion from Mars: A study in the psychology of panic*. Princeton: Princeton University Press. (Original work published 1940).

Carey, J. W. (1992). *Communication as culture: Essays on media and society*. New York: Routledge.

Cram, P., Fendrick, M. A., Inadomi, J., Cowen, M. E., Carpenter, D., & Vijan, S. (2003, July 14). The impact of a celebrity promotional campaign on the use of colon cancer screening: The Katie Couric effect. *Archives of Internal Medicine, 63*(13), 1601–1605.

Czitrom, D. J. (1982). *Media and the American mind: From Morse to McLuhan*. Chapel Hill: University of North Carolina.

Disney plans to omit film scene after teenager dies imitating it. (1993, October 20). *New York Times*, p. A21.

Downing, J. D. (Ed.). (2004). *The Sage handbook of media studies*. Thousand Oaks, CA: Sage.

Downing, J. D. & O'Connor, A. (1995). Culture and communication. In J. D. Downing, A. Mohammadi, & A. Sreberny (Eds.), *Questioning the media: A critical introduction* (pp. 3–22). Thousand Oaks, CA: Sage.

Eagleton, T. (1991). *Ideology: An introduction*. New York: Verso.

Eagleton, T. (2000). *The idea of culture*. Malden, MA: Blackwell.

Ferrel, J. (1995). The politics of wall painting. In J. Ferrel & C. R. Sanders (Eds.), *Cultural criminology* (pp. 277–294). Boston: Northeastern University.

Fiske, J. (1989). *Reading the popular*. New York: Routledge.

Gardner, R. & Shortelle, D. (1997). *From talking drums to the Internet: An encyclopedia of communications technology*. Santa Barbara, CA: ABC–CLIO.

Geertz, C. 1973. *The interpretation of cultures: Selected essays*. New York: Basic Books.

Gilmore, R. W. (1993). Terror austerity race gender excess theater. In R. Gooding-Williams, *Reading Rodney King/Reading urban uprising* (pp. 23–37). New York: Routledge.

Graber, D. A. (2007). Introduction. In T. M. Schaefer & T. A. Brickland (Eds.), *Encyclopedia of media and politics* (p. xxvii). Washington, DC: CQ Press.

Griffith, R. (1970). Foreword. In H. Münsterberg, *The film: A psychological study* (pp. v–xv). New York: Dover.

Grossberg, L., Nelson, C., and Treichler, P. (1992). *Cultural studies*. New York: Routledge.

Hall, S., Clarke, J., Critcher, C., Jefferson, T. & Roberts, B. (1978). *Policing the crisis: Mugging, the state and law and order*. London: Macmillan.

Herman, E. S. & Chomsky, N. (1988). *Manufacturing consent: The political economy of the mass media*. New York: Pantheon Books.

Herzog, G. (1964). Drum signaling in a West African tribe. In D. Hymes (Ed.), *Language in culture and society* (pp. 312–323). New York: Harper & Row. (Original work published 1945).

Hoggart, R. (1957). *The uses of literacy: Aspects of working-class life with special references on publications and entertainment*. London: Chato and Windus.

Huesmann, R. L. & Eron, L. D. (Eds.). (1986). *Television and the aggressive child: A cross-national comparison*. Hillsdale, N.J.: Lawrence Erlbaum Associates.

Inglis, F. (1990). *Media theory: An introduction*. Oxford, UK: Basil Blackwell.

Jordan, A. L. (2008). Broadcasting yourself (and others): How YouTube and blogging have changed the rules of the campaign. *Hinckley Journal of Politics, 9*, 75–84. Retrieved May 24, 2009, from http://www.hinckley.utah.edu/publications/journal/index.html.

Levine, L. (1990). *Highbrow/Lowbrow: The emergence of cultural hierarchy in America*. Cambridge, MA: Harvard University.

Littlejohn, S. W. & Foss, K. A. (2005). *Theories of human communication* (8th ed.). Belmont, CA: Thomson Wadsworth.

Locke, M. (2005, February 21). "Hooray for Hollywood" say pinot noir producers. *USA Today*. Retrieved July 22, 2009, from: http://www.usatoday.com/money/industries/food/2005-02-21-pinot-noir-sideways_x.htm.

Macdonald, D. (1965). Masscult and midcult. In *Against the American grain* (pp. 3–75). New York: Vintage.

MacLeod, D. V. L. (2004). *Tourism, globalization and cultural change: An island community perspective*. Clevedon, UK: Channel View Publications.

Martín-Barbero, J. (1993). *Communication, culture and hegemony: From the media to mediations*. London: Sage.

Masterman, L. (1994). *Teaching the media*. London: Routledge.

McChesney, R. W. (1999). *Rich media, poor democracy: Communication politics in dubious times*. New York: The New Press.

McDermid, C. (2007, July 13). Michael Richards finds inner solace in Cambodia. *Los Angeles Times*, http://articles.latimes.com/2007/jul/13/entertainment/et-richards13

McManus, J. H. (1994). *Market-driven journalism: Let the citizen beware*. Thousand Oaks, CA: Sage Publications.

McQuail, D. (1994). *Mass communication theory: An Introduction* (3rd ed.). London: Sage Publications.

McQuail, D. (2004). Overview of the handbook. In J. D. Downing (Ed.), *The Sage handbook of media studies* (pp. 1–16). Thousand Oaks, CA: Sage.

Mead, G. H. (1934). *Mind, self and society*. Chicago: University of Chicago Press.

Merriam-Webster's Collegiate Dictionary (11th ed.). (2005). Springfield, MA: Merriam-Webster, Inc.

Münsterberg, H. (1916). *The film: A psychological study*. (Original title: *The photoplay: A psychological study*). New York: Dover.

Park, R. E. (1922). *The immigrant press and its control*. New York: Harper & Brothers.

Payne, A. (Director). (2004). *Sideways* [Motion picture]. United States: Fox Searchlight Pictures.

Peirce, C. S. (1991). *Peirce on signs: Writings on semiotics*. Chapel Hill: University of North Carolina Press.

Picard, V., Stearns, J., & Aaron, C. (n.d.). *Saving the news: Toward a national journalism strategy*. Available from the Free Press. Retrieved June 23, 2009, from http://www.freepress.net/media_issues/journalism.

Postman, N. (1985). *Amusing ourselves to death*. New York: Viking Press.

Pratkanis, A. & Aronson, E. (2000). *Age of propaganda: The everyday use and abuse of persuasion*. New York: W. H. Freeman and Company.

Rosaldo, R. (1989). *Culture and truth: The remaking of social analysis*. Boston, MA: Beacon Press.

Saussure, F. de. (1959). *Course in general linguistics*. New York: McGraw-Hill.

Schudson, M. (1978). *Discovering the news: A social history of American newspapers*. New York: Basic Books.

Sklar, R. (1994). Movie-made America: A cultural history of American movies. New York: Vintage Books.

Starkman, D. (2009, May/June). Power problem: The business press did everything but take on the institutions that brought down the financial system. *Columbia Journalism Review*, 24–30.

Tahmincioglu, E. (2007, October 5). The quiet revolution: Telecommuting. Retrieved May 6, 2009, from http://www.msnbc.msn.com/id/20281475/.

Thompson, E. P. (1963). *The making of the English working class*. New York: Pantheon.

Ward, D. S. (Director). (1993). The program [Motion picture]. United States: Samuel Goldwyn Company.

Williams, R. (1960). *Culture and society, 1780–1950*. New York: Anchor Books.

Williams, R. (1981). *The sociology of culture*. Chicago: University of Chicago.

Wines, M. (1993, October 21). Reno Chastises TV networks on violence in programming. *New York Times*, p. A1.

CHAPTER 3

Issues and Challenges

This chapter addresses some of the issues and challenges many writers experience when writing about the media, such as finding trustworthy information, selecting a topic, and planning one's research and writing. The chapter begins with an overview of the main challenges of writing a successful media paper followed by a section designed to help writers identify reliable sources. Next, the writing process is covered, including information on how to select a topic or work with the one that is assigned and how to use a research journal and a schedule as tools to manage one's writing and research. To help writers with their research and writing, sample schedules, along with numerous writing tips, are provided. The chapter concludes with the discussion of plagiarism and ways to avoid it. While in this chapter, for clarity of exposition, strategies for finding reliable sources, keeping track of one's progress, and making a research and writing schedule are discussed as distinct and consecutive steps, writers should keep in mind that working on a media research paper or professional report is not a linear process. Instead, research and writing strategies often overlap, making the actual writing process less straightforward.

OVERVIEW OF MAIN ISSUES AND CHALLENGES

The first challenge a writer encounters is that of finding a trustworthy body of prior research. Because the value of a research paper or professional report rests to a large extent on the quality of its sources, the importance of finding and relying on rigorous and methodologically sound studies cannot be overestimated. Weak sources, such as popular blogs or opinion pieces, cited in a research paper or report will lead the reader to question any conclusions the writer makes. Thus, finding reliable sources is perhaps the most important challenge any writer encounters.

Finding current information is another challenge. Academic books and journal articles, generally considered the most reliable sources of media information, are usually a few months, if not years, behind the times. This is because academic publications require collecting and analyzing data, writing up and verifying results, receiving and incorporating suggestions from other researchers—all time-consuming but necessary steps. In contrast, more popular magazines and newspapers are current but less reliable. In most research papers and professional reports, it is important to include both current and older sources that have withstood the test of time. The reason for going back to such works is that oftentimes what appears to be a new event or development turns out to be a recurring theme. For example, media writers Nichols and McChesney (2009) promote the idea that news media, specifically newspapers, should receive government subsidies. They base their argument on the fact that the news media play an important role in informing the public about government and business affairs. Many would consider such a suggestion new. In fact, subsidizing the production and distribution of information goes back to the early days of the colonial period. The establishment of the postal system is one example of a government subsidy for news media. The U.S. Postal System was set up primarily to distribute news and information, not personal correspondence (Cook, 1998, chap. 3). Reading about the history of newspapers in the U.S. can contribute to the understanding of an issue like that of subsidizing the news media. But while the idea of subsidizing newspapers may not be new, the conditions under which news is produced today are certainly different from the conditions that existed over 200 years ago in colonial America. Classic studies about the colonial press and current studies on the production of news today can provide a more comprehensive view of the issue.

Another challenge for many writers is selecting a topic. Recall from Chapter 2 that media studies encompass a broad range of issues and topics. Some media writers find it hard to decide on a topic. In this chapter the process of selecting a topic is introduced and later, in Chapter 5, elaborated on further.

It is important to keep in mind that writing about the media, like most writing, is best described as a spiral, rather than a linear process, because writers continuously change and revise their ideas. Writers go back and forth in their research and writing. Rather than following an orderly process that starts with finding a topic, researching the topic, and then writing the paper, the actual process of writing can take many twists and turns before the paper is finished. This less-than-direct route is a major challenge to many writers. Indeed, the paradox of writing a paper lies in the linear or orderly form of the finished product—a polished paper—and the zigzag process of producing it.

It is because of this seemingly haphazard route to writing and research that the importance of planning the research and writing phases cannot be stressed enough. While the process of working on a media paper is not linear, writers still have to approach their assignment in a disciplined manner. Making a schedule, keeping track of progress, and working steadily toward the goal of a finished paper or report are often the difference between the finished paper or report and the one that cannot seem to get off the ground. Reading, understanding, and following the guidelines below can dramatically increase the writer's chances of successfully completing a research paper or report.

IDENTIFYING RELIABLE SOURCES

One of the first observations a media writer makes when starting to research a media topic is that there are all kinds of sources of information that are easily accessible. The challenge lies in finding reliable information. The Internet is a great resource that has made it possible to access a tremendous amount of information in a matter of seconds. This resource, like all other resources, has pluses and minus. On the plus side, a wealth of information is readily available.

Knowledgeable people who follow a process, or research method, that promotes an objective and balanced view of a topic produce some of this information. Sound research methods allow for opposing views to be included in a research paper and both their strengths and weaknesses acknowledged. Researchers who respect this process are willing to let others critique their assumptions, findings, and methods.

The downside about information found via the Internet is that much of it is erroneous, inaccurate, and incomplete. Many people and organizations with a cause to promote produce information that is far from balanced or fair. Consciously or subconsciously, these people or organizations tend to skew information to support their cause or ideas. While the Internet is a great equalizer in terms of providing access to information, it is not very good at sifting through that information to separate the good from the bad.

How is a media writer to sort through this maze of information? There are steps that can be taken to improve one's chances of tapping into reliable sources of information. The phrase "improve one's chances" should not be interpreted as a "guarantee." Therefore, it is always a good habit for a researcher to maintain a healthy dose of skepticism when searching for and consulting sources. Most problems related to questionable sources begin when writers let their guard down.

It is important to keep in mind that the writer's objective is to find the *best* information, not the *most* information. With regard to sources for a media paper, quality trumps quantity every time (Rubin, Rubin, & Piele, 2005, p. 89). Fifteen to 20 well-selected, highly reputable sources listed on the Works Cited or References list of a paper or report carry much more weight than a hundred mediocre sources.

Developing a sense for separating good research from poor research is a skill that improves with practice. Yet there are some basics about distinguishing between solid references and weaker ones that every media writer should learn from the start. The first, already mentioned, is to develop a healthy sense of skepticism. A skeptical attitude is difficult to nurture because it requires writers to step outside their comfort zone and question what has been accepted as common sense. Take, for example, the question of media bias. Some studies demonstrate that the media are biased toward the liberal side of the political spectrum. Other studies show that the media are biased toward the conservative side of the spectrum. The organization FAIR (Fairness and Accuracy in Reporting, www.fair.org) advocates for more balanced coverage of controversial issues. FAIR was started in the mid-1980s by persons who believed the news media were tilting toward the right. Another organization, AIM (Accuracy in Media, www.aim.org), was founded by people who believe that the media are too liberal. Which is correct? Which is more reliable?

Another hot button issue has to do with media violence. Do the media promote violence in society? Again, some studies indicate that they do, while others indicate just the opposite (Gunter, 1994, pp. 167–168); still others show that the media may not have an effect in terms of violence in society. Some studies demonstrate that children who are exposed to violent acts on television will imitate those acts (e.g., Bandura, Ross, & Ross, 1963). In a laboratory setting, a child watching someone strike a Bobo doll on television, for example, is found to be more likely to take a swing at a Bobo doll.

Critics of experimental research about media violence (Freedman, 2002; Sparks, 2006, p. 86) point out that what happens in a laboratory setting may not transfer into the real world. A child may know from previous experience that, unlike a Bobo doll, another child may cry or swing back, or a teacher or parent may punish aggressive behavior. Other critics point out that family background and parental behavior may have a stronger influence than a television program, movie, or video game. Families that discourage violent behavior and model nonviolent behavior may have more influence on their children than a television program or video game.

Given the amount, and often conflicting, information available, how is a student, or someone otherwise new to writing about the media, to evaluate sources of information? There are five points that a writer should keep in mind when evaluating sources of information (Rubin et al., 2005, pp. 36–38):

1. the author's standing in the scholarly community
2. the publisher's reputation

3. the issue of objectivity
4. the accuracy of the information
5. the currency of the information

In the following section, these five points are examined in more detail.

The first point in determining the reliability of a source is credibility of the author of a book or article (Booth, Colomb, & Williams, 2008). If the author is a well-known expert in the field of media research, the researcher should expect the publication to be credible and of high academic quality. Aristotle called this type of credibility "ethos," which means the expertise and reputation of the author convinces the audience that the information can be trusted. For instance, in the area of international communication, the name Annabelle Sreberny-Mohammadi—the author of several books and peer-reviewed academic journal articles on the topic and one of the leading specialists in the field—helps to identify a publication by this author as reliable.

When a media writer starts doing research in any field, determining who the reputable scholars are is understandably challenging. The following are some basic questions that can help in this process. Is the writer of the book or journal article someone on the faculty of a college or university? Does the writer have academic credentials, such as a PhD, JD, MD, or some other degree that indicates that she or he has been vetted by the academic community? If the writer is not affiliated with a college or university, is he or she affiliated with a reputable organization, such as a nonpartisan research group or institute? It is also a good idea to ask what other publications the writer has produced. This answer can be tricky as the number of published works does not automatically indicate their quality. However, scholarly books, as well as peer-reviewed academic journals published by national or international organizations, generally have the highest ranking among scholars, followed by academic journals published by regional or local organizations.

When glancing over a book that is being considered as a source, writers should pay attention to the name of the publishing company. The publisher of a book or the organization sponsoring a journal should have the respect of the academic community it serves.

Books published by university presses are usually held in high regard. Books published by large, profit-driven corporations tend to be ranked lower in terms of academic prestige. Earning respect depends on several criteria. One issue to consider is whether the publisher has a history of publishing works of importance in the field of media studies. Many times, but not always, such publishers are affiliated with a college or university. University presses continue to be seen as being more committed to publishing important works of scholarship.

However, university publishers are not the only ones who enjoy good reputations. Some publishers not affiliated with universities specialize in academic manuscripts. Publishing houses such as Bedford/St. Martins, Routledge, Sage, Westview, and Wiley have good reputations for producing scholarly texts even though none are affiliated with a college or university. Organizations such as the Wilson Institute in Washington, DC, and the Project for Excellence in Journalism (part of the Pew Research Center), are examples of organizations that are not associated with a university—although many, if not most, of their research staff hold doctoral degrees—but publish highly regarded reports and other scholarly publications.

Writers should keep in mind that there is nothing wrong with asking professors or other experts in the field of media studies for assistance in determining the quality of sources. Academics often ask one another about what journal articles or books to read when starting to research a new field or area of study. In addition, because academics are highly trained, they can look at a scholar's publications and make a general assessment of the quality of that scholar's work. The book publisher(s) with which a scholar is associated, the journals where he or she publishes, and the sources a scholar cites, all provide clues to the quality of an author's work, clues that can be easily overlooked by a student or someone new to the field. Asking for help from professors or experts with the evaluation of sources is perfectly legitimate, especially when starting to research a new media topic.

Another issue to consider when searching for reliable sources is that of fairness or balance. Many media researchers question the idea of objectivity. It is unlikely, these researchers argue, that a person can somehow forget his or her values, beliefs, and ideas at the moment that a research project starts and be completely impartial. All persons are part of the culture in which they are nurtured. This means absorbing the values, beliefs, and ideas of the culture. To expect a researcher to "switch off" his or her values, beliefs, and ideas and assume a completely neutral stance on an issue is unreasonable.

So what is a media writer to do? It is best to admit one's own biases, acknowledge one's own beliefs, and be aware of one's own ideas and feelings about media issues. Once these biases are recognized, the media writer should make every effort to present as many points of view on a topic as possible. The media writer should strive to find those books, journal articles, Web sites, and other sources of information that present two or more sides of an issue in a rational and respectful manner. In addition, the media writer has an obligation to actively seek and find information from different sources, even ones that are diametrically opposed to the views the writer may hold. Such views should be acknowledged, briefly summarized, and respectfully critiqued.

In the process of scrutinizing sources for reliability, the date of publication should not be overlooked (Booth et al., 2008, pp. 78–79). For many areas of media research it is crucial that sources, especially secondary sources, be current. Using up-to-date sources demonstrates the researcher's knowledge of current trends and the latest theories in media research. It makes the researcher's case more believable. Academic journal articles, while they may take a year or two to appear in print, are the most current and trusted forms of information in the field of media studies. Books written by one or two authors are usually written over a long period of time, about a year or longer. The actual writing of a book may have been preceded by several years of research. Edited books may be put together by one or more editors who first select a theme or issue to be addressed in the book and then select either previously printed, or new, articles by different contributors to appear as chapters in the book.

While currency of information is important, this does not mean that seminal works in the field should be excluded. Complementing current sources with the "classics" can only strengthen a paper's argument. The classic works in media studies, which, given the history of the field, can include Aristotle, Freud, Marx, Hegel, and many others. Familiarity with classic sources, and referencing them in media papers when appropriate, can give a paper depth that will be appreciated by readers. Including such sources demonstrates that the writer knows the long history of the media topic under discussion and can put it in a historical context.

Writing Tip: Beware of citing sources for the sake of citing sources. Reference to a source should move the argument of a paper forward. To cite ancient Greek or Roman philosophers just for the sake of citing them will not be appreciated by readers. One of the reasons for submitting a draft of a paper early is to have the reviewer evaluate the appropriateness of sources. A good reviewer will not only recommend that a source or two should be included, but will also recommend that inappropriate sources be eliminated.

As stated above, reliable sources are publications by those researchers who have a track record of serious study in their area(s) of expertise. Publications may be articles in academic journals, books, or chapters in books, published by university presses, and reports produced by university-affiliated institutes, private institutes, government agencies, or other organizations, such as professional societies. Can writers be certain that the sources they cite are correct? They cannot. At best, a source can be approved by a scholarly community. But if the scholarly community's assumptions are faulty, so too will be the findings of a research project. Studies have shown that errors do appear in journal articles and books, and reviewers of publications will often point out errors made by authors and overlooked by publishers. In one extreme case, known as the "Sokal Hoax," Sokal fabricated an entire article. He wrote it in the most obscure language possible and submitted it for publication in *Lingua Franca*, where it was accepted. Only later did Sokal reveal that the entire article was a hoax. (See "The Sokal Hoax," the eds. of *Lingua Franca*, 2000).

The following list of questions is designed to help media writers navigate their way through the amount of information that is available to them and select those sources most likely to be reliable:

1. Is the journal article, book, or Web site the product of a reputable press? (Is it published or maintained by a university or college press? If not, does the press have a reputation for publishing academic books and monographs? If an organization is publishing the book or report, what is the reputation of the organization? Does it have the respect of the scholarly community?)

2. Is the book or journal article peer reviewed? (Have other scholars read and approved the work? A university press or scholarly community that publishes a journal will typically submit manuscripts for review by recognized experts in the field who will advise the publisher or editor on whether or not the submission meets academic standards for publication. Many publishing houses not affiliated with a university or academic organization also send books out for review by a community of scholars.)

3. Is the author a reputable scholar? (What other books or journal articles has he or she written? Who published those books or journal articles? Has the name of the researcher been spotted in the list of references of the other works that have been consulted?)

4. If the source is online, is the site sponsored by a reputable organization? (What is the position of the sponsoring organization on the issue(s) addressed? When was the site last updated? Is there a "Who We Are" page on the Web site? Is there a "Contact Us" page on the Web site?)

5. Is the information current? (When was the article or book published? When was the information posted online? When was it last updated?)

6. If the source is a book, does it have notes and a bibliography? (A book without citations or a bibliography should make the media writer reconsider using such a text. This is usually an indication that the work is not sufficiently serious for consideration as a scholarly publication. However, if it is a rare source that provides valuable firsthand information, can the information be corroborated by other sources?)

Learning to evaluate sources takes some time, but over the course of learning this skill, certain names, publishing houses, and organizations and their reputations will become familiar. With time, evaluating sources, will become second nature.

The items included in the list above should serve as a reminder of how important sources are for a media writer. A research paper, essay, or report will only be as good as the sources used to answer a research question or examine a media issue. For this reason, the evaluation of sources should be given ample time and attention.

A word of caution: Once a writer is comfortable with certain sources, there is a tendency to keep going back to the same ones. This habit can blind the writer to new and exciting discoveries in the field of media studies. Such new and exciting discoveries can invigorate one's writing. Recall what was mentioned before about actively searching for opposing views. The same applies to new views. Media writers should actively seek out new and unique perspectives and evaluate them. This assures that the writer remains current and is aware of new developments in the field.

CURRENCY OF INFORMATION

Because of the rapid changes in media technologies and the diffusion of those technologies among the general population, one of the problems unique to media writers covering cutting-edge inventions and new media developments is finding sources that include current information. There is usually a lag between the time a manuscript is presented to a publisher and when it is printed and distributed to bookstores. As noted earlier, it is not unusual for a book or journal article to take up to two years to appear in print from the first time it is initially submitted to an editor for review.

Trade publications, such as *Columbia Journalism Review*, *American Journalism Review*, *Wired*, *Broadcasting and Cable*, and other monthly and weekly magazines are more current, but have not undergone a strict review process that academic books and journal articles usually undergo. One way to stay current in the field without compromising the quality of information is to read articles in magazines like the ones listed here by writers who have a record of other publications. If a magazine writer has one, two, or three books and several academic journal articles in print, and has recently written a magazine article in her or his area of expertise, then that information is probably reliable.

Similarly, one can do an Internet search of respected academic writers and visit their Web sites to see if they have posted information on a particular research topic. A scholar who investigates media violence, for example, may have a recent posting on his or her blog (e.g., see MIT professor Henry Jenkins's "Reality Bytes: Eight Myths about Video Games Debunked," at http://www.pbs.org/kcts/videogamerevolution/impact/myths.html).

THE WRITING PROCESS

As mentioned earlier, writing about the media requires that the writer select a media-related topic, research the topic, and write the paper. At first glance, this three-step process appears fairly simple and straightforward. However, writing about the media is usually anything but simple or straightforward. For most researchers, even some of the most experienced, it is a formidable challenge. This is why, in addition to following these three steps, a well-written research paper or report requires that the writer plan ahead and invest enough time to complete the writing project by deadline.

While the steps outlined herein appear to be neat and orderly, the process of writing a paper can be unruly. For example, after locating and reading articles on the selected topic, the writer might have to go back and revise his or her preliminary outline or search for more books and articles. Even when putting the final touches on a research paper, one might find that a quote is missing or is cited improperly, which may mean going back to the library to locate the source and verify the information. All researchers experience these types of problems.

Another important issue to keep in mind is deadlines. While researchers should strive to write and submit the best work possible, part of the challenge is to complete the research paper or report in a timely manner. Late work, even if it is of high quality, may be either rejected or given a lower evaluation than it deserves. Many professors, for example, will not accept late work. At the workplace, supervisors will grow impatient with writers who miss deadlines. Thus, writers should keep in mind that it is important to strike a balance between perfection and completion. As Williams (2007), an expert on research and writing pedagogy, observes, "perfection is the ideal, but a barrier of done" (p. 9). Starting early and working consistently and methodically are key components of writing an excellent paper and finishing it on time. For the media writer, starting early, planning ahead, and working steadily are challenges that, when met, will pay off handsomely.

WHAT EXACTLY IS THE ASSIGNMENT: WRITER'S CHOICE OR ASSIGNED TOPIC?

The first order of business when writing about the media is to find out if the topic of the research paper or report is "open" or if it has been selected. If "open," it is important to know just how open the topic is. Most professors will give students a choice in the selection of a topic so long as it remains within the parameters of the course. In the workplace, however, supervisors tend to assign a specific topic to a staff member.

In an academic setting, students should check with the professor who is teaching the class to make sure that an appropriate topic for research has been selected. It would be a mistake to proceed to do research and start writing about a topic before the professor approves it. A simple e-mail to the professor informing her or him of the selected topic will suffice, unless a more formal proposal is required. What may seem like an appropriate topic to the student, especially first- and second-year college students, may not be considered appropriate by the professor. Managers and supervisors typically provide specific information about what is to be addressed in a written report. In some ways, an assigned topic makes starting the writing process easier. After all, the writer can jump right in without spending time looking for a topic to write about. As soon as the topic is assigned, the writer can proceed to the research phase of the project.

Checking with the professor or paying close attention to the request made by a supervisor is related to the point raised earlier in the book about considering the audience. While the primary audience is either the professor or the supervisor, a writer should construct the paper as if addressing an intelligent but uninformed reader. This means defining terms, explaining concepts, and avoiding overuse of professional jargon. Such writing will be more coherent and demonstrate the writer's grasp of key concepts.

As mentioned earlier, some professors and editors may assign a specific topic or suggest a general area of study from which the idea for a paper should originate. More commonly, a professor will allow some leeway in the selection of a topic so long as it falls within the parameters of the topic of the class. For example, in a class on the history of print, a professor is likely to allow research papers on such topics as Johann Gutenberg (who is often credited with inventing the printing press), the influence of the printing press on politics, the relationship of the printing press to the Renaissance, censorship in Europe after the invention of the printing press, the role of inexpensive books and newspapers in the shaping of a national identity, and the rise of printing as an economic and political force in society. A topic such as the introduction of illustrations or photos in newspapers and books would also be acceptable. Even the introduction of computer-generated texts may be a viable topic as it links old and new printing technologies. All of these topics, and others too numerous to list, would likely be acceptable in a class covering the history of print. But it is still important to check with the professor to make sure that the topic is acceptable.

While the assigned topic allows writers to escape the pressure of selecting a topic, its downside may be a lack of affinity for a topic as opposed to one that is personally selected. This is why most books on how to write research papers suggest that, whenever possible, writers select a topic that interests them. Having a topic assigned may deny the writer this opportunity. However, it may be that some writers who are assigned a topic may be among the lucky ones who like the suggested topic. But what should a writer do if he or she has no interest in the topic that was assigned? There are three options.

First, the writer can learn to like the assigned topic. This is not as farfetched as it sounds. Just like taking a class to fulfill a requirement sometimes turns out to be an enjoyable experience, so to writing about an assigned topic may turn out to be a real pleasure. The writer might discover a new and exciting area of research that he or she wasn't aware of previously. It is best to be open-minded. If a topic has been assigned, give it a chance and maintain a positive attitude. After all, plenty of people seem to enjoy writing about the topic. Perhaps there is something to the topic that will be discovered in the process of researching and writing about it.

It is also possible that a new perspective on the topic may be seen from the vantage point of an outsider. Many discoveries have been made by persons from outside a field of study who were able to see old data, or patterns, in new ways. For example, Philo Farnsworth had no formal training in physics or engineering when, at age sixteen, he developed a system for electronic television (see Barnouw, 1990). Unfamiliarity with a topic can be turned into a strength.

Most important, a writer should not get discouraged and let the unfamiliar or uninteresting topic affect the quality of his or her research and writing. As stated earlier, the topic could become interesting at any stage of the writing and research project. Stranger things have happened. So at least be open to the possibility that an assigned topic that initially causes psychological discomfort may by the end provide for a very positive and rewarding learning experience.

Second, if trying to like the topic doesn't seem to be working, try talking to the professor. After letting him or her know why the assigned topic, which is perfectly good and fine (remember that this may be the professor's area of expertise, which means he or she finds it interesting enough to write about!), is not working, offer an alternative topic that is still *well within* the parameters of the class. This is not the time to argue for a topic that is on the margins. Do some homework before the meeting and show up prepared with a topic, a paragraph or two about the topic, and some references. If you are taking a course on films of the classical Hollywood period, for example, don't suggest writing a paper on Quentin Tarantino's *Kill Bill*, Vols. I & II (Tarantino, 2003, 2004). In fact, it's a good idea to google the professor and find out what areas of media studies she or he has written about. The professor may be more likely to allow a change in topic if it is one in which she or he is interested.

A third option is to stick with the assigned topic, treat it with respect, write the research paper, and move on. Writing about some topics is enjoyable and writing about others is not. Be a professional, do the assignment, and make the best of an uncomfortable situation. Above all, remember that when doing research and writing about the media, many things can happen along the way to a finished paper. Being happy with a topic at the start of a research project is no guarantee of being happy with the topic later in the research process. Just like writers who find that an assigned topic they had no interest in turns out to be fascinating, many writers grow tired of a topic they once looked forward to researching. More than a few graduate students putting the final touches on their theses and dissertations will readily admit that they are ready to move on to a new topic.

Another point to keep in mind is that selecting one's own topic does not necessarily mean that the process of writing will be easier than when the topic is assigned. It is common for novice writers to identify a topic of research only to find that their interest changes as they begin to investigate the topic. This is actually a normal part of the writing process. In the process of carrying out research, the writer's appreciation for the subject matter deepens, which often leads to the refinement of the initial topic. Reevaluation of original ideas, while it may be frustrating to inexperienced writers, is actually welcomed by more experienced writers as a sign of solid research practices.

Another common challenge for those who choose their own topic is that, about halfway through the writing process, many writers experience the feeling that they have selected the wrong topic. This happens because the enthusiasm associated with finding a research topic usually begins to fade as the writing assignment progresses—some sources seem impossible to locate, while the sources that have been found, instead of providing answers, raise new questions about the research topic, requiring a rethinking and sometimes even rewriting of the original research question and outline. With some frustrations beginning to surface, the idea of changing one's topic becomes very tempting. Resist the temptation.

Being overwhelmed by the problems one encounters at the beginning of the writing process is typical and even expected and is not necessarily an indication that the wrong topic has been selected. In fact, the chances of selecting the wrong topic are actually very low. In most cases it is best to continue to research and write about the topic that has already been selected, introducing some modifications as the writing process moves ahead. Next are suggestions and strategies to help writers overcome some of the issues and challenges that arise on the way to a finished research paper or report.

PRELIMINARIES

In order to take full advantage of the time available to write the paper and get the most out of the research experience, it is important to have a plan that includes a timeline. Such a plan of action should also include keeping a record of the sources and ideas that will make up the final paper. Research is challenging, complex, and often makes writers reevaluate their original ideas. Because good research usually leads to the reshaping of one's original ideas, enough time should be set aside for a thorough job of researching and writing. Although initial ideas may seem a bit rough, it is still best to write them down. While they may seem unrefined at the time, later, as the research process unfolds, one or two of those ideas may develop into highly polished gems.

Another reason for putting ideas on paper is that many times the act of writing disorganized thoughts helps crystallize them. This is because writing tends to be more formal than speaking. Verbal communication is filled with informal grammar, unfinished sentences, and sudden changes in focus and topics. When talking to others, people depend on facial expressions, gestures, tone of voice, and other signs to communicate their thoughts. Such cues help flesh out the verbal message being communicated.

Unlike verbal communication, written communication is removed in time and space from the audience, who relies on grammar, spelling, punctuation, and a clear explanation to understand the intended meaning. Furthermore, written communication is more formal, and therefore requires more discipline. This is why, in the process of writing thoughts on paper, they tend to come into sharper focus. Getting into the habit of recording ideas on paper or on a computer is advantageous because it advances the research project and makes it more manageable.

RESEARCH JOURNAL

Because putting thoughts on paper helps clarify one's thinking, it is strongly suggested that detailed notes be kept in the process of collecting information from books and articles and from discussions with professors and peers. Such notes can be handwritten, but writers will save time if they keep their research records as computer documents. Save the notes on both a hard drive *and* a flash drive. Label the flash drive with your name, university or department, and phone number or e-mail address.

It is also a good idea to get into the habit of e-mailing research notes to one's e-mail address. At the initial stages of research, e-mail the notes (either as attachments or as text in an e-mail message) every week. As the pace of research and writing picks up, e-mail the notes and rough drafts at the end of every day. Creating and keeping an electronic folder in an e-mail account with e-mail messages that contain sources, ideas, rough drafts, comments from readers, and any other information related to the writing assignment is another way to make sure information is not lost. If a computer crashes, or a laptop is lost or stolen, or if a flash drive is misplaced, the information can still be retrieved from an e-mail message. Attaching research notes, and later drafts of the paper to e-mail messages is a way to avoid the embarrassing situation of having to tell a professor or boss that the paper or report cannot be delivered on time because of a computer crash, theft, or misplaced flash drive.

Indeed, the one excuse a writer does not want to use before the paper is due is that information, or data, was lost. There are multiple ways to back up information to ensure that, in the event of an unfortunate incident, data do not disappear. Keeping a research journal, electronic or hardcopy, is the best way to back up information. Save all of this information at least until a research paper has received a grade or a supervisor has approved a report.

If there is no access to a laptop computer or the writer prefers taking notes in the old-fashioned, but very reliable, method of using paper and pencil, make notes in a simple spiral notebook. Again, the writer's name, the name of the writer's university, department, or place of work, and office telephone number or e-mail address should be on the cover of a new notebook. Include the phrase: "If found please return." Contact information clearly visible on the front cover of the notebook means that if the writer leaves the notebook in the library, computer lab, subway car, or coffee shop, there is a chance someone will return it. Without contact information, there is no chance that the notebook will ever be returned. After writing notes and ideas in the research journal, researchers should transfer the notes on to a computer and save them as a Word document. As soon as possible, preferably later that evening, researchers should e-mail the saved notes to themselves.

Writing Tip: Do not use single sheets of paper for recording research notes. The reason is simple—single sheets of paper can be easily lost. Too much time and energy is invested in research efforts to risk losing valuable information.

Writing Tip: Do not spend a lot of money on notebooks, pens, or paper. Most professors and supervisors are not impressed with fancy, leather-bound notebooks or 25 percent cotton paper. What they are impressed with are the ideas and the quality of the writing used to express those ideas. Make a trip to the local office supply store or discount store and pick up a package of notebooks and some ballpoint pens. The same goes for the paper used to print the essay or report. A package of recycled, white, 8 × 11 paper will do just fine. There is no need to spend money buying high quality paper. We, the writers of this book, have never met professors who give extra points for the quality of the sheets of paper an essay is printed on. The professors we know grade the quality of the ideas in the paper and not the monetary value of the sheets of paper. Do, however, avoid colored paper or unusual sized paper. Also, use black ink for all writing assignments. Blue, green, or some other color ink is not only unprofessional, but can be annoying as well. Many professors simply refuse to read research papers that are not printed in black ink and on plain white paper.

A word of caution: Do not confuse the advice to use inexpensive stationery products with approval of a messy presentation. When the final

paper is submitted, make sure that the pages are numbered and arranged
in order and do not have any food spots.

When writing information in a research journal, always include the dates entries are made, full name of the author or authors whose work is being read, full titles of books or articles, the title of the source journal, the year the books or articles were published, the city in which a book was published, the name of the publisher, and the page number(s) where the information was found. In sum, it is prudent to write more rather than less: Having too much information will not cause an additional trip to the library, while not enough information will. This information will come in handy when constructing the list of references for the research paper or report. If you photocopy a page from a book or a journal article, write the reference information on the back of the copy.

Additionally, terms and definitions one comes across in the course of research should also be included in the research journal. While reading the chapters in textbooks and going over the glossary and index, make notes of those terms, names, and ideas that are interesting and that may be included in the final research paper.

RESEARCH JOURNAL NOTES

In addition to the previous information, the research journal should also include the writer's notes or evaluations of the books and articles that are being read. What is the key point of the article? What methods of data collection and analysis did the author use? What is the author's point of view? Why does the author take the position that he or she does? What arguments are made? What evidence is presented for and against the author's argument? What are some of the weaknesses of the author's argument? What are the strengths?

This information will be invaluable at the writing stage because it demonstrates to readers that the writer has critically evaluated someone else's writing on the subject. Writing research journal entries should be taken seriously—be accurate, careful, and fair. Because of time constraints, one might not be able to go back and reread the original documents, but must instead rely on the collected research notes.

When taking notes, avoid copying entire paragraphs or pages from the books or articles. The reason for not copying entire paragraphs of text is that too often, under pressure to finish a paper and turn it in, a writer may forget what he or she wrote and what was copied from a book or article. Such an error can lead to accusations of *plagiarism*, which is copying someone else's work and passing it off as one's own (see following discussion of plagiarism). Plagiarism is an accusation to be avoided at all costs. If some pages from a book or a journal article must be copied, use a copy machine. This guarantees that the information is accurate and that it will not be confused with one's own ideas and observations. If a paragraph or two from an article or book must be copied by hand, clearly indicate the cited material with quotation marks, and include the author's full name(s), journal or book title, article title, city of publication and publishing house, and page numbers. Other additional coding strategies, such as using different colored ink, can be used to indicate that these entries were copied from someone else's work. Using a highlighter with an unusual color can also help in such situations. The point is to code or identify direct quotations in some way that marks them differently than the writer's paraphrasing, comments, or observations on a text.

Keeping a research journal takes a little getting used to at first, but the researcher will soon come to appreciate the effort. While it may seem time consuming in the initial stages of the research phase, the information recorded in the journal will save the researcher time and energy later in the writing phase. It is important to remember the old saying, "taking time saves time." A record of the research process can help solve many—not all—of the problems that may arise at the later stages of the writing process. If a question arises about a reference, the information can be easily located in the research journal. A quotation, definition of a term, or name of an author that needs to be checked can be found in the research journal notes. While it takes some discipline to keep a research journal, it can pay dividends later in the research and writing process, especially for the writer just starting to learn how to write about the media. Planning your work is another strategy for successfully writing about the media that also illustrates the wisdom of the saying "taking time saves time."

PLAN YOUR WORK

A major challenge for many media writers is meeting a deadline. Even writers with years of experience sometimes have difficulty finishing a project on time. Planning ahead is the key to meeting this challenge. The process of writing a research paper or professional report will be much smoother, more efficient, and satisfying if a writer has a plan. Is it possible to write a research paper or report without a plan? Yes, but a researcher is more likely to encounter problems without one. Without a plan, the likelihood of experiencing high levels of anxiety and frustration increases. Investing a little time in a research plan can help minimize such feelings. A plan can also save the researcher time later in the research and writing stages. Ultimately, it leads to a more rewarding writing experience and better final product.

Knowing when the paper or report is due is crucial to planning a research project. Students should read the class syllabus to find out when the paper is due. Media professionals should also know the exact date for delivering the paper. Once a deadline is known, the writer should work backwards to the present to plan a research schedule. Some professors provide their students with specific target dates for the process of writing a research paper: when the paper outline is due, when a list of references or bibliography is expected, and when a rough draft is to be turned in. If no such target dates are given, as in the case of most professional reports, the writer should create such a schedule and resolve to stick to it.

Writing Tip: Team up with a fellow student, or students (but no more than three), and keep each other motivated by (1) meeting in the library once a week or once every two weeks and (2) e-mailing progress reports to each other on scheduled dates. This is similar to going to the gym with an exercise buddy. You are more likely to show up at the gym or the track if you are meeting someone there. The same is true with research and writing. Like exercising, research and writing are easy to put off. Coordinating with two or three other persons can provide the added incentive necessary to work on a paper or report consistently. Many cities and towns have writers' groups that meet regularly to read and critique one another's work. Knowing that someone else will show up at the meeting with two or three pages for the others to read is great motivation for everyone in the group to also write two or three pages.

Why limit the group to four people? In our experience, the writing group tends to lose focus when more than four people come together. The writing group is not a social gathering, but a task-oriented group. Socializing may happen, but only after work has been read and critiqued.

A schedule for researching, writing, and revising should begin with the first day of class, or, for a media professional, from the day the responsibility for writing a report is assigned. A key decision at this point is whether and when to turn in a first draft of the research paper to the professor or supervisor for suggestions and comments. There are good reasons for doing this. Providing the professor or supervisor with a first draft of the research paper or report allows him or her to raise any concerns about the paper before the deadline. In general, the earlier problems in a paper are identified, the better. Turning in a paper on deadline only to find out it does not meet the standards set by the professor or supervisor (in content, format, style, or some other criteria) leaves no time to make corrections. Giving persons who will pass judgment on the paper a preview is one way to avoid serious problems further down the road, when it may be too late. For example, suppose that while reading a draft of a research paper a professor notices that one of the authors cited has been misinterpreted. A note in the margins of the paper, an e-mail, or face-to-face discussion with the student can resolve the problem. In another scenario, the professor may realize that an author who has made an important contribution to the area of media studies that is being covered in the paper has been overlooked. The professor may recommend a book or journal article that will give another perspective on the topic. Any feedback from professors or supervisors, ranging from suggestions about the organization of the paper to identifying weaknesses in the paper's argument, can only make the final paper stronger.

Receiving a lot of comments and suggestions should not lead to discouragement. Comments and suggestions are an indication that the reader (audience) is interested in the topic of the paper or report and willing to invest some time and effort toward its improvement. Rather than get discouraged, the writer should patiently, and diligently, address each comment and suggestion.

By planning ahead and giving professors and supervisors a first draft of a paper or report, many problems and oversights can be taken care of before the final version of the paper is due. If some professors or supervisors do not accept first drafts for review, writers may instead submit an outline of the paper, which is usually shorter, but nonetheless gives an idea of the main point of the paper and its supporting evidence (for more information about outlines, see Chapter 4).

START EARLY

A key element in any strategy for writing a good media research paper, or any research paper for that matter, is to start early. Avoid procrastination at all costs. It sounds simple and may even seem obvious, yet, for many students, and even some professional writers, this first hurdle is one of the most difficult to clear. Many students, and not a few media practitioners, put off their writing projects as long as they can. Usually the result of such procrastination is an inadequately researched and poorly written paper. Starting early means that the day the research paper is first mentioned is the day to start thinking about an appropriate topic. It is also the day to start thinking about a strategy for writing and researching the paper or report. (See previous writing tip about joining a writer's group.)

A well-researched and well-written media paper is not likely to be written overnight. In general, the more time allocated for the paper, the better. Starting to work in September on a research paper due in December may seem odd at first, but such an approach will prove to be of great benefit. Starting early allows the writer to work on the media research paper slowly, steadily, and methodically, which will be reflected in the pages of the final version of the paper.

The biggest mistake many writers make is that they procrastinate. Putting off the media research paper assignment or report until the week before it is due, or even worse, the night before it is due, is a mistake too many good students and media practitioners make. Good papers take time to research, organize, write, and rewrite.

Many students believe a professor will not be able to tell the difference between a paper that was researched and written the night before and one that was researched and written over the course of the semester. Actually, it is quite easy to distinguish between the two. A professor will know immediately when a writer rushed to produce a research paper. The formatting will be either incorrect or inconsistent. There will be typos and misspellings throughout the text. Grammatical mistakes will appear frequently. The hurried research paper will be poorly structured. The introduction will not be focused. The paper will lack a clear thesis sentence. In the body of the paper, the writer will be "all over the map." Quotations, which should rarely be more than a sentence or two, will be too long because the writer is trying to fill the required number of pages. For the same reason, the fonts tend to get a little larger and the margins wider. Citations will lack details, such as the publisher's name or city where the book was published, or will be absent altogether. All of these problems reflect poorly on the writer. It is very difficult for a professor to consider awarding a student a passing grade or for a supervisor to accept a report when so much is obviously wrong with the submitted work.

Some people believe that because writing comes easily to them they can quickly and effortlessly write a media research paper. However, it is important to keep in mind that there are different types of writing, and being good at one of them does not guarantee being good at all of them. Writing a research paper is not like writing a long e-mail message to a friend. Nor is it like writing an in-class essay or an essay that expresses an opinion on a certain topic. An in-class essay or an opinion piece differs from the media research paper in several ways.

The purpose of the in-class essay is to assess how well the student grasps the topics presented in the textbook and in class lectures. The grade for an in-class essay is based on how the student answers the question within a limited time period, sometimes as little as 20 minutes, but more likely 45 minutes to an hour. The in-class essay asks for the student's informed view or perspective on a particular topic. It evaluates the student's ability to weave arguments logically, support a point of view, and express thoughts on the topic clearly.

Much the same may be said about writing an opinion piece about the media. An opinion piece is relatively short compared to a research paper and asks for the writer's *informed* point of view on an issue or topic. In contrast to an in-class essay, in an opinion piece the writer is expected to voice his or her own thoughts on the topic. Ideas expressed in the writing should be clear and logical and the essay coherent. That is, like other types of writing, it should present a clear idea, a thesis statement in the first paragraph, which lays out what the reader (always remember the audience) can expect in the rest of the essay. In the paragraphs that follow the thesis statement, the arguments of the writer should be presented along with supporting material. Finally, a conclusion that ties the points made in the paper to the ideas presented in the introductory paragraph should give the essay a satisfying ending that provides the reader with a sense of closure.

In sum, a research paper differs from the in-class or opinion essay in length, scope, and structure. First, the research essay is much longer than the in-class essay. For instance, most professors require that a research paper be in the range of 10–15 pages, which translates into roughly 3,000–4,500 words. Second, unlike the limited time and scope of both the opinion piece and the in-class essay, the research paper demands that a topic be thoroughly researched and that the findings be reported in a detailed fashion. Because of the limitations of time and length, the in-class essay, as well as the opinion paper, can be more general than the research paper. The content of the research paper should reflect the amount of time and effort invested in its development. Third, while the in-class essay and the opinion-piece move into a discussion quickly, the research paper requires that the writer present insights on the topic only after acknowledging the findings, opinions, and insights of other researchers who have made significant contributions to the academic discussion that is the focus of the research paper. Moreover, in a research paper or professional report, writers are expected to support any statements they make with examples gleaned from the research literature or data. In addition, and in contrast to the more relaxed style and format requirements for the in-class writing assignment or the opinion essay, a media research paper should be formally written and properly formatted. Think of the first two as a sprint and the research paper as a marathon—both require somewhat similar skills, but different strategies.

Quality papers are well researched and well written over a reasonable period of time. Poorly written papers are usually slapped together at the last minute. Allocate enough time not only to writing the paper but also to rewriting it. Such efforts will be reflected in the pages of the paper or report.

WHEN IS THE PAPER DUE?

An important consideration when selecting a topic and scheduling the different stages of the writing process (deciding on a topic, researching the topic, writing, and revising the manuscript) is how much time a writer has to complete the research paper. In today's academic environment, the length of a "semester" can vary.[1] While many colleges and universities still offer classes that take an entire semester, or about 16 weeks, some accelerated degree programs offer classes that take half that time. Pay close attention to how many weeks there are from the first day the research paper is assigned to the day the paper is due. Designing a research-and-writing schedule that allows for the maximum time to work on a paper is critical. The time available will, to a large extent, determine the length of the paper.

During a 16-week semester, a student will probably be asked to write a paper that is anywhere from 10 to 15 double-spaced pages. During a shorter semester, for example an eight-week session, a student may be expected to write a shorter paper, eight to 12 pages, but not necessarily one that is less scholarly or professional. During the shorter semester, it is reasonable to limit the number of books, journal articles, and reports to review, because there simply is not enough time to collect and analyze extensive materials. Research will have to be more focused and selective. Less time makes designing a manageable schedule even more important.

Another important part of the research-and-writing schedule is allowing time for unexpected setbacks. As stated earlier, the writing process does not follow a linear progression. There will be setbacks, and writers should allocate time for the unexpected. For example, a journal article may not be available in the library. A book may be checked out or lost. A journal containing an important article may be anywhere in the library except its assigned shelf. It is possible that an article once available online is no longer accessible via the Internet. In such cases, it becomes necessary to fill out a request for library staff to conduct a search for the book or journal article. Such a search may take a few days, perhaps even weeks. If time for the unexpected has been worked into a writing schedule, it is easier to deal with such a delay. If the book or article does not turn up after a few days, the next course of action is an interlibrary loan request.

Writing Tip: There are many reasons why a book or journal article may not be on the shelf of a library. It could be lost. It may be misplaced—that is, slipped into the wrong shelf by mistake. If so, request that the source be traced. Books and journals may also be out for binding. Binding can take weeks, if not months. While most libraries do a good job of keeping books on the shelves, never assume that library materials will be available when they are needed.

Every library has a procedure for ordering books from other libraries. Ordering journal articles online is easier, since the article is e-mailed in a PDF format to the e-mail address of the person who requests it. Receiving hard copies of books or journal articles from other libraries can take anywhere from three to 10 days. So in addition to starting early, be sure to allow time for locating hard-to-find sources. Check with the reference librarian to find out how to order journal articles that are not available in the library and how long it will take to receive them. A research-and-writing plan can help the writer stay on schedule and meet the deadline for the assignment. It provides a gauge of the writer's progress and lets him or her know when the project is likely to be finished. The great benefit of a plan is that it provides a course of action that the writer can use to complete the assigned task successfully. The old saying, "plan your work and work your plan," applies when writing research papers.

DEPEND ON PERSPIRATION NOT INSPIRATION

Some novice writers object to planning their work. This objection is sometimes based on the belief that planning, especially long-term planning, robs them of their spontaneity and creativity. These writers prefer to rely on "inspiration," "the Muse," or some other force they believe will allow them to write research papers in one sitting. They are in for a big surprise. Rather than depend on inspiration, it is best to rely on professional habits. A professional is someone who gets the job done on time, whether inspired or not.

Meeting the challenge of writing a good research paper that will earn high marks or a professional report that will attract the attention of supervisors requires a consistent and methodical approach. There will be setbacks, but these are best handled in a calm, deliberate fashion. If a schedule has been properly designed, there will be time to take care of unexpected problems and delays. On the other hand, when writers discover that sources they need are checked out, misplaced, or simply not available a few days before the paper is due, they are more likely to panic—never a good state to be in when trying to compose a well-thought-out, coherent research paper. Starting early and having a plan for the research-and-writing project increase the chances of working consistently over time to finish a high-quality paper or report by deadline. Coming up with a research-and-writing schedule should be part of a strategy for any writing project. A schedule not only helps keep the project moving forward, but also helps the writer develop a professional attitude toward research and writing.

CONSTRUCTING A SCHEDULE

The following section offers three sample schedules. Writers can use them as guides to construct their own schedules. The purpose of such schedules is to help the media writer reach the goal of completing a research paper or professional report. It is important that every writer come up with a schedule that suits his or her individual needs and particular circumstances. For example, those persons fortunate enough to live where there is access to an excellent library or libraries will need less time for library research. Excellent libraries, such as large state and private university libraries and large municipal libraries, tend to have large reference sections, subscribe to numerous journals, and may have multiple copies of books. These large libraries also tend to have more resources, such as electronic databases, CDs,

DVDs, and special collections. Smaller schools often have libraries with fewer resources. When using a small library, writers should allocate more time for requesting books and receiving journal articles through Internet requests or interlibrary loans.

Having access to experts in the field may also affect the research-and-writing schedule. College students should consult professors. If a professor's name comes up as the author of an encyclopedia article on the topic being researched, or if the professor is known in the field because of a book or paper on the topic, by all means contact him or her. However, it is important to be professional in such encounters. If contacting the professor via e-mail, use an institutional or professional e-mail address. In e-mail communication, avoid typos, informal language, and abbreviations. Do not send the professor your draft with requests for review, unless the professor asks for it. If the professor agrees to a meeting, be sure to read the book or paper that she or he has written on the research topic to be discussed before sitting down for an interview. It is also advisable to have a list of questions to ask. At the end of the interview or discussion, be sure to ask for the names of other professors on or off campus who may have some knowledge about the topic under discussion, as well as a list of recommended readings.

Planning a work schedule includes breaking down the timeline for researching, writing, and revising the paper. For example, if there are 16 weeks until the paper is due, as in the first sample schedule, dedicate a week or two to preliminary research. The purpose of this preliminary research is to find a topic (see Chapter 5). Use the "countdown" method for scheduling research activities. The benefit of the countdown method is that there is never any doubt of how much time is left before the paper is due.

SAMPLE SCHEDULE #1: THE IDEAL
Week 16
Attend the first class, or meeting, and make notes about what the professor or supervisor expects in the research paper. Read the syllabus carefully to determine which topics may be appropriate for a research paper in that particular class. After class, take a few

minutes to review the textbook. Pay close attention to chapter titles, information boxes, and key words, and mark interesting points that may be molded into a research paper topic. Some textbooks even have sections titled "Suggestions for Research Projects." Do not feel compelled to follow such suggestions, but do not overlook them either.

Week 15

In the research journal, go over the initial notes made while thinking about a topic for a research paper or professional report. Go online to find out what books and journals are available in the campus or municipal library and what resources, such as government documents and reports by research institutes, are available via the Internet. This is also a good time to tour the university library and talk to a librarian about the library's media holdings. Select a general topic, and get it approved by the professor or supervisor. Draft a thesis sentence.

Writing Tip: Look for both pros and cons to include in a research paper. Rather than being afraid of information that contradicts the paper's thesis, seek it out. This will not only make the paper stronger, but it will also make it more interesting to read.

Week 14

With preliminary knowledge about the paper's topic, revise the thesis sentence and write a rough outline of the paper. Don't worry about formal outlines at this point. (More information about how to write outlines, along with a few samples, can be found in Chapter 5.)

Week 13

Start to write a rough draft of the paper. Do not worry about the number of pages. What is important at this point is that some effort be invested in starting to write the paper. Pay attention to the time it is taking to put ideas on paper, and use this information to pace the entire project.

Week 12

Return to the university's online library and Internet sites, such as Google Scholar, JStor, and EbscoHost, and look up more sources to fill in any gaps in the paper's arguments. Continue writing a rough draft of the paper.

Week 11

Revise the outline and thesis sentence based on the latest research. Continue writing a rough draft of the paper.

Week 10

Finish a rough draft of the paper.

Week 9

Prepare a "clean" first draft for presentation to the professor or supervisor. A "clean" first draft means that it should be as close to the final draft as possible. There may be a missing page number, or year of publication for a citation, that still needs to be tracked down, but otherwise the paper should be close to the final draft.

Week 8

Turn in the first draft to the professor or supervisor for suggestions and comments.

Week 7

Get the first draft back from the professor and discuss the sources (including films, audio recordings, newspaper stories, etc.), arguments, and bibliography.

Week 6

Look up any research materials suggested by the professor or supervisor, and address his or her comments and suggestions.

Week 5

Include new information in the revised version of the paper.

Week 4

Prepare the final draft of the paper.

Week 3

Check the documentation and style of the paper, and correct grammar and spelling errors.

Writing Tip: At this point in the writing process, most writers are so familiar with what they have written that it is easy to overlook mistakes, even some obvious ones. What is needed is a "fresh" pair of eyes to read the paper in order to identify and correct mistakes. We advise that roommates, friends, or relatives not be asked to read the paper, unless they can be trusted to be mercilessly honest. Most roommates or friends are not comfortable declining a request to read a paper, but neither are they comfortable giving criticism. Relatives usually cannot say no, either, and it may be hard for them to be critical as well. It is better to go to the university's writing center or academic center and meet with a writing counselor. Another option is giving the paper to one of the members of the writing group.

Week 2

Turn in the final draft to the professor or supervisor.

Week 1

If the professor or supervisor finds an unexpected problem with the paper (formatting issue, missing pages or references), it can be corrected during this week.

SAMPLE SCHEDULE #2: THE REAL

Most students give themselves about two or three weeks to write a research paper. Obviously, most professors believe three weeks is too short a time span for a quality research paper or report, especially if students work and have a full class schedule. It is strongly suggested that students and professional writers give themselves a minimum of six weeks to write a research paper or report.

Week 6

Come up with a topic, get it approved by the professor or supervisor, and begin online and library research. Write a rough outline and a thesis statement.

Week 5

Write a rough draft of the research paper. Notice what parts need work. Where are the gaps in the paper's arguments that need to be filled? Make notes of how much research still needs to be done. Also, see if the writing needs work. Make an appointment with the writing/academic center.

Week 4

Do more research to flesh out the research paper, and polish the writing. Set the paper aside for a couple of days.

Week 3

Reread the paper, and determine if one more trip to the library or additional online research is needed to smooth out rough edges in the paper. For example, where are the gaps in the argument? What points made in the paper could use more support in terms of evidence (results of surveys, statistics, etc.)?

Week 2

Work on final draft. Check documentation and style of paper and correct grammar and spelling errors.

Week 1

Turn in the final draft.

SAMPLE SCHEDULE #3: "I WAITED TOO LONG!"

(One-week schedule)

Day 7

Decide on a topic, and get it approved. Don't make it too narrow. Head to the library and check the shelves and academic journals. Go online for information.

Day 6

Write a rough draft from start to finish.

Day 5

Review the rough draft, make corrections to the text, and note any gaps in the arguments that require more research/information.

Day 4

Return to the library and/or do online research for data that can make the paper's argument stronger.

Day 3

Rewrite the paper with added information.

Day 2

Prepare the final version of the paper. Proofread and format it properly.

Day 1

Turn in final version of paper or report, and promise to start earlier next time a paper is assigned.

When following a 16- or six-week schedule, develop a study routine that allocates three to five hours of research and writing per week. As the research and writing move along, decide whether adjustments to the writing schedule are necessary (for more on research schedules, see George, 2008). Fast writers may find that research is taking longer than expected and so may allocate more time for finding and reading sources. Slower writers may have to budget more time for writing. Other factors, such as experience and familiarity with the topic, should also be taken into consideration when adjusting the research-and-writing schedule. A first-year student new to the campus and not familiar with the library's resources may need more time to get oriented. Some large state universities have several libraries on campus. A junior or senior who has used the library for a couple of years should be more familiar with the system. Students who work full-time will need to consider how their work schedule will impact their research and writing.

Beware, however, of faulty assumptions that lead one to believe that someone with experience writing research papers and reports will have an easier time than someone without such experience. For example, a college senior may convince himself or herself that less time is necessary for writing a research paper than when he or she was a first-year student. Such logic, however, does not always rule over the research paper writing process. Many experienced writers, even those with years of experience, report having just as hard a time as when they wrote their first paper. In fact, the process may get harder because one's own standards get higher and the level of competition gets tougher. Seniors are judged by a different standard than first-year students because they are compared to those students who, like themselves, have survived to compete in the fourth year of college. A standout paper in a first-year college-level course may not distinguish itself among papers written by fourth-year students.

Writing Tip: Although it is best to start early, it is never too late to construct a writing schedule.

Begin working on a research paper or report by scheduling time for preliminary research and writing a thesis sentence. Many novice writers, especially first-year students, do not realize how much time solid research can take. Searching through electronic catalogs, looking for books and journal articles, skimming materials, making photocopies, jotting down notes, and requesting books and articles through an interlibrary loan system all take time. Starting early will give the media writer an idea of how much time it takes to research a topic and provide a sense of how to pace one's work. Research is best done without undue pressure, which tends to make one anxious and, consequently, often results in sloppy note taking, research, and writing. With time on their side, writers tend to be more relaxed and thus able to pay more attention to details in the writing-and-research process.

Starting early also allows one to get a handle on what resources—books, journals, trade magazines, CDs, DVDs, speeches, interviews with experts in the field, Web sites—related to the topic are available. Learning that some of the resources will be almost impossible to get does not have to be a tragedy. If enough time has been allotted, the topic can be reshaped to work with the sources that are available. One of the worst feelings a writer can experience is the sense of doom that comes with finding, after putting off researching and writing the paper or report until a week or two before it is due, that most of the materials needed are either in a special collection in a private library halfway across the country or checked out from the local library and that it will take at least a week to recall them.

Writing Tip: An advantage to starting research early is that, at the beginning of the semester, most library books, journals, and other sources will still be on the shelves. Near the end of the semester is when more books get checked out and journals are misplaced. Part of the research-and-writing process is learning early in the process what resources are available.

Although this point has been made before, it cannot be stressed enough that starting early is a key ingredient in the development of a successful paper or report. The writing process is fraught with roadblocks and detours. These are unavoidable. Starting early is the only way to deal with setbacks in a calm manner that allows the media writer to focus on the final goal, that is, the finished paper or report.

Writing Tip: The beginning of the semester is also the time when librarians are not overwhelmed with requests. A reference librarian can help with a search by showing the researcher relevant electronic databases, refining the search, and assisting with the acquisition of off-campus materials. However, near the end of the semester, when students line up to ask for help, a librarian can dedicate only very limited time to each patron. Again, it is to the writer's advantage to start work early.

WRITE FROM THE START

A key factor in learning how to pace oneself when writing a research paper or report is to write every day. Even writing only half a page per day will give the media writer an idea of how much time it actually takes to get thoughts down on paper. Novice writers are often surprised by how long it takes to "translate" ideas that seem so clear in their head into logical, coherent statements on a page.

Writing and research should be done simultaneously. Approach writing as a way of thinking out loud on paper. Research guides writing, and writing guides research. It is only when writers put their ideas on paper that they become fully engaged in critical thinking.

Avoid the mistake of believing that the paper can be written only after *all* of the research and thinking about the topic has been done. There will always be that one article or book that cannot be found; there will always be the desire to rewrite a sentence or paragraph. Do not let the frustration of not finding one or two sources hold back the writing project. If fine-tuning a sentence or paragraph seems to be leading to a complete restructuring of the paper, it is best to stop and have someone else read the paper. If an objective reader, such as a professor, writing counselor, or editor, asks for reasonable changes, by all means make them. Then turn the work in and focus on the next project.

In a linear understanding of the writing process, a topic should first be researched, and then a paper written based on that research. In reality, the steps in the process are less straightforward. As writers conduct research, they may get ideas that need to be written down. As they write, they may find that there are gaps in the arguments presented in the paper. As noted before, writing guides research, and research guides writing.

Keeping a research journal is helpful in this regard. In addition to keeping a record of sources and ideas, a journal can be used to keep notes that may be included in the final version of the research paper. Fleshing out ideas on paper gives the writer some perspective on the topic. After a few days or a week, what initially seemed like perfectly good ideas may begin to look like incoherent statements, while a side remark noted in the research journal may develop into the core argument of a research paper. This is exactly why it is suggested that a writing project be started early.

PLAGIARISM

Plagiarism is a word students hear early and often in college. This is because it is a serious issue on college campuses today. It is also a serious issue in the professional world. To plagiarize is "to steal and pass off (the ideas or words of another) as one's own: use (another's production) without crediting the source" (*Merriam-Webster Collegiate Dictionary*, 2005, p. 946). Plagiarism is unethical and, if the material being plagiarized is copyrighted, illegal. It is unethical because the words and ideas being used are actually the result of someone else's thinking. Not giving proper credit to the person or persons who first introduced those thoughts is considered theft. Plagiarism is also illegal because, at least in the United States and several other countries, intellectual property, like other types of property, is legally protected. Taking another person's words, ideas, photos, graphs, and other creations without giving proper credit is a violation of copyright laws (www.plagiarism.org/plagirarism.html).

It can also be considered fraud, because the plagiarist is presenting himself or herself as the person who came up with the original ideas or words, when in fact they were "stolen" from someone else. The word *plagiarism* comes from the Greek word *plagios*, which means kidnapper ("What is Plagiarism and How to Avoid it," 1999). Thus, a plagiarist is someone who abducts the words and ideas to which others have given birth.

Researchers accused of plagiarism tend to fall into two categories. There are intentional plagiarists and unintentional plagiarists (Owl at Purdue, http://owl.english.purdue.edu/owl/resource/589/01/; Booth et al., 2008, pp. 191–192). Intentional plagiarists are those who knowingly and willingly set out to turn in, and take credit for, a paper they did not write. Such individuals may buy papers from companies that trade in research papers. Intentional plagiarists may also belong to a campus organization such as a fraternity, sorority, or some other club, where they may help themselves to one of the papers that other members of the organization have collected and are willing to "share" (Booth, Colomb, & Williams, 2003, p. 201; Storch & Storch, 2002). Intentional plagiarists also take sentences and ideas from multiple sources and assemble "their" papers by cutting and pasting.

Unintentional plagiarism is when a researcher unwittingly fails to provide citations for the words and ideas he or she took from someone else's paper, book, journal article, or Web site. Unintentional plagiarism is often the result of sloppy and rushed work. Intentional or unintentional, for students, plagiarism can be grounds for penalties ranging from an F on the research paper assignment to expulsion from school; for media practitioners, plagiarism can result in disciplinary action, including losing one's job.

The Internet facilitates plagiarism because it is easy to copy information from different Internet Web sites and compose a paper by pasting the information into a Word document. However, this is neither research nor writing. While in high school, when asked to write about a topic, such as President Roosevelt's fireside chats, some students were allowed to go to an encyclopedia Web site and copy the information on Roosevelt's fireside chats word for word and turn in the report without any repercussions. The rationale behind such high school assignments is that copying sample texts will eventually lead to improved writing skills in the student. However, it is important to remember that college is not high school (Georgetown University Honor Council, "In My Country/High School . . .," n.d. http://gervaseprograms.georgetown.edu/honor/system/53508.html).

Some international students accused of plagiarism argue that in their country or culture it is a sign of respect to copy the writings of a wise person. Different ideas about what constitutes intellectual property can further muddy the waters regarding intercultural perceptions about plagiarism (see reference to Georgetown University Honor Council, "In My Country . . .," above.). It is important for such students to follow the requirement of the program—the U.S. academic program—that they choose to be a part of. (See section for ESL writers in Chapter 5.)

Many honest and hardworking students have trouble determining what is and is not plagiarism. It can be confusing, especially for undergraduate students just getting started on their first college-level research projects. As stated at the beginning of this book, one of the best ways to avoid plagiarism is to start writing and researching a paper early in the semester. Oftentimes students give in to the temptation of plagiarism because as the deadline for the paper approaches and they start to research their topic, they realize that the amount of time needed to write the college-level research paper exceeds the time they have left before the paper is due. By starting early, students give themselves enough time to plan a strong research paper, allow for the gestation of ideas, and the writing and revisions that a high-quality research paper requires. Starting early also allows time to ask the professor, or staff member at the university's writing center, questions about proper citation. Starting early and working consistently and methodically is the best way to avoid the temptation of plagiarism.

WHEN SHOULD A WORK BE CITED?

There are several rules every media writer should know regarding proper citation. The first rule is that when copying a sentence or two from a book, journal article, newspaper, or some other source, it is necessary to either place the copied sentence in quotation marks, or, when the cited material exceeds four lines, block the quoted sentence(s) from the rest of the text. It is also required to let the reader know who wrote the passage, the year it was published, and the page number(s) from which it was taken. Later, in the References or Works Cited section of the paper, a complete citation should appear. If a writer fails to cite properly, she or he can be accused of plagiarism.

For example, when writing a research paper on the growth of the music channel MTV, a researcher writes the following: *MTV has been the most successful U.S. cable exporter. In 2005 MTV launched its one hundredth export offering. MTV Europe alone had 45 regionalized channels with nine targeted solely at the United Kingdom; MTVE had dedicated offerings that included MTV Romania, MTV Nordic, and MTV Russia.*

This passage in italics would be a clear case of plagiarism because the writer has not given the reader any indication—such as quotation marks, the name of the author, year of publication, or page numbers—that this information was found in Tunstall's (2008) *The Media Were American: U.S. Mass Media in Decline* (p. 102). Quotation marks are one way of alerting the reader to the fact that information was taken, word for word, from a book, article, or some other text.

Another way of alerting the reader that this is a direct quote is to block the quoted material if it is longer than four lines of text, from the rest of the research paper, as is done in the following example. In addition to blocking the quote, however, the writer needs to provide information about where the quote can be found.

This is done by including the author's last name, the year the book or article was published, and the page number(s) where the quote can be found. At the end of the paper, in the References or Works Cited section, the full citation would be given:

> MTV has been the most successful U.S. cable exporter. In 2005, MTV launched its one-hundredth export offering. MTV Europe alone had 45 regionalized channels with nine targeted solely at the United Kingdom; MTVE had dedicated offerings that included MTV Romania, MTV Nordic, and MTV Russia. (Tunstall, 2008, p. 102)

What if the student doesn't want to quote directly, but instead wants to paraphrase what Tunstall wrote? Would she or he still be obligated to provide a citation? Yes. The second rule is that all information gathered during the research process, even if paraphrased, needs to be cited. The previous quote, when paraphrased, needs to be rewritten as follows: *According to Tunstall (2008), MTV's presence around the world, including its nine channels in the United Kingdom, as well as its channels in Romania, Russia, and Sweden, make it the leading U.S. cable exporter (p. 102).* Paraphrasing an author's ideas does not relieve the researcher of the obligation to give the author credit. Not to do so would be considered plagiarism.

The third rule has to do with what is referred to as "common knowledge." It is not necessary to provide a citation for information that is generally known. The problem is in determining what information is generally known. What is common knowledge to one person may not be to another. This is where one's research experience becomes important. According to Purdue University's Writing Lab (1995–2009), as a rule of thumb, if the same information has appeared without attribution in five or more sources, it is *probably* common knowledge and does not require a citation. Another way to determine if information is common knowledge is to ask if the information is known to readers. Finally, if someone can easily find the information using general reference materials, it is probably common knowledge. Communication and media studies professors can help in determining if a piece of information is common knowledge in the field of media studies.

For instance, in writing about the development of wireless telegraphy, it would be important to review the impact of the sinking of the *Titanic*. In discussing this tragedy, it would not be necessary to give a citation for the year of the sinking of the *Titanic*, 1912. This is because many people know the year, or if they don't know the exact year, they can easily find out. Most persons in the field of media studies are familiar with the date because of the effects the sinking of the *Titanic* had on the development of wireless telegraphy in the U.S. Soon after the *Titanic* went down, Congress voted to pass the Radio Act of 1912, requiring that licensed radio operators be on board every ship and limiting amateur radio operators to shortwaves (Starr, 2005, p. 219).

When writing a paper on political communication and the rhetorical strategies used by John F. Kennedy during his inaugural address, a writer does not need to produce a citation for the phrase, "Ask not what your country can do for you, ask what you can do for your country." It is common knowledge that President Kennedy made that statement during his inaugural speech in 1961. However, the phrase itself should be enclosed in quotation marks.

The fourth rule for avoiding plagiarism is to develop good note-taking strategies. Good note-taking skills are extremely important because they save writers time and prevent plagiarizing other people's work. Sometimes, while taking notes, a researcher may not clearly mark his or her comments from the material copied from the original text. Weeks later, especially if under the pressure of a deadline, it is very easy to forget which were one's own comments and which were quotes or ideas taken from someone else's work. A good way to distinguish between one's own ideas and those of others is to put big quotation marks around the material taken directly from sources (see previous discussion on page 58–59 for more suggestions on note-taking). A writer should get into the habit of synthesizing material as it is being read. After reading the introduction to a journal article or book, put the text aside. Open the research notebook and try to explain in a brief paragraph, four or five sentences, what the author was trying to communicate. In this way, the media writer is paraphrasing the ideas in the text. However, paraphrases, similar to direct quotations, also require attribution. This strategy is one way of making sure that when writing a paper, the writer does it in his or her own voice and not that of the authors that have been consulted.

Finally, the fifth rule to remember is to err on the side of caution. If not sure whether to cite or not, cite (Purdue University Writing Lab, 1995–2009). The consequences of citing when it is not required are minor compared to those of not citing when it is necessary. Why take the chance?

There are several excellent Web sites to help students and media practitioners navigate through the citation maze and avoid the plagiarism trap:

CollegeBoard.com   http://www.collegeboard.com/article/0,3868,2-10-0-10314,00.html

Georgetown University Honor Council (1999). What Is Plagiarism? Online: *Georgetown University Honor Council Web Site*. URL: http://www.georgetown.edu/honor/plagiarism.html (July. 1, 1999).

Howard University Library. Information and Research Assistance Guides: Plagiarism. http://www.howard.edu/library/Assist/Guides/Plagiarism.html

The pamphlet *Acknowledging the Work of Others*, prepared by the Office of the Dean of Faculty, Cornell University, September 2006.

The Writing Lab & The Owl at Purdue, Purdue University. (1995–2009). "Is it Plagiarism Yet?" Retrieved June 4, 2009, from http://owl.english.purdue.edu/owl/resource/589/02/

http://owl.english.purdue.edu/handouts/print/research/r_plagiar.html

Plagiarism.org http://www.plagiarism.org/plagiarism.html

Turnitin.com http://www.turnitin.com/

Trinity Washington University. Academic honesty, plagiarism, and the honor system. http://www.trinitydc.edu/policies/honesty_plagiarism_and_honor_system.php

SUMMARY

Writing a media research paper or report is a process that requires a plan of action, knowledge about the field, and an understanding of the research and writing process. In this chapter, several issues and challenges that every media writer encounters have been addressed. These issues and challenges can be summed up as time, sources, and topic selection.

The key to finishing a research paper or report on time is to start early. Writers can adapt one of the three sample research and writing schedules presented in this chapter to meet their deadlines. Media writers should note their own working habits and design a schedule that best suits their individual needs and assignments. Once the writing assignment is received, a writer needs to allocate enough time for research, writing, and rewriting. A good schedule is one that keeps the writer on track up until the day the paper is delivered.

Reading textbooks, academic books, scholarly journals, and trade magazines is the best way to stay abreast of the latest findings related to one's topic. This is also a good way to learn who the leading scholars are in the field. With time the media writer will become familiar with the concepts, terms, and history of the topic.

Selecting a topic for a paper or report can be a daunting task for media writers because, as was pointed out in Chapter 2, the area of media studies offers a broad spectrum of topics for research and writing. While the challenges of selecting a topic and delivering a paper on time are introduced in this chapter, strategies for producing a successful media research paper will be explored in Chapter 4. At this point it is important to realize that paying close attention to the parameters of the course or the assignment is one way to begin narrowing the topic so it can be covered in a manageable research paper or professional report.

NOTE

1. The word *semester* comes from the Latin *semestris*, which means "half-yearly." The Latin word *sex* means six—thus six months (mensis). Academic years used to be divided into two, six-month periods. (Semester. [2009]. In Merriam-Webster Online Dictionary. Retrieved May 8, 2009, from http://www.merriam-webster.com/dictionary/semester.)

REFERENCES

Bandura, A., Ross, D., & Ross, S. A. (1963). Imitation of film-mediated aggressive models. *Journal of Abnormal and Social Psychology, 66,* 3–11.

Barnouw, E. (1990). *Tube of plenty: The evolution of American television.* New York: Oxford University Press.

Booth, W. C., Colomb, G. G., & Williams, J. M. (2003). *The craft of research* (2nd ed.). Chicago & London: University of Chicago Press.

Booth, W. C., Colomb, G. G., & Williams, J. M. (2008). *The craft of research* (3rd ed.). Chicago & London: University of Chicago Press.

Cook, T. E. (1998). *Governing with the news: The news media as a political institution.* Chicago: University of Chicago.

The editors of Lingua Franca (Eds.). (2000). *The Sokal hoax: The sham that shook the academy.* Lincoln: University of Nebraska Press.

Freedman, J. L. (2002). *Media violence and its effects on aggression: Assessing the scientific evidence.* Toronto, Canada: University of Toronto Press.

George, M. W. (2008). The elements of library research: What every student needs to know. Princeton, NJ: Princeton University.

Georgetown University Honor Council. (n.d.). In my country/high school, using someone else's work is a sign of respect." Retrieved June 4, 2009, from https://www11.georgetown.edu/programs/gervase/hc/plagiarism.html#Country.

Gunter, B. (1994). The question of media violence. In J. Bryant & D. Zillman (Eds.), *Media effects: Advances in theory and research* (pp. 163–211). Hillsdale, NJ: Lawrence Erlbaum Associates.

Merriam-Webster's Collegiate Dictionary (11th ed.). (2005). Springfield, MA: Merriam-Webster, Inc.

Nichols, J. & McChesney, R. W. (2009, April 6). The death and life of great American newspapers. *The Nation,* pp. 11–20.

The Purdue online writing lab. (n. d.) Retrieved June 10, 2009, from http://owl.english.purdue.edu/owl/.

Rubin, R. B., Rubin A. M., & Piele, L. J. (2005). *Communication research: Strategies and sources* (6th ed.). Belmont, CA: Thomson/Wadsworth.

Sparks, G. G. (2006). *Media effects research: A basic overview.* Belmont, CA: Thomson/Wadsworth.

Starr, P. (2005). *The creation of the media: Political origins of modern communications* (2nd ed.). New York: Basic Books.

Storch, E. A. & Storch, J. B. (2002, June) Fraternities, sororities, and academic dishonesty. *College Student Journal.* Retrieved July 23, 2009, from http://findarticles.com/p/articles/mi_m0FCR/is_2_36/ai_89809975/.

Tarantino, Q. (Director). (2003). *Kill Bill: Vol.1* [Motion picture]. United States: Miramax Films.

Tarantino, Q. (Director). (2004). *Kill Bill: Vol.2* [Motion picture]. United States: Miramax Films.

Tunstall, J. (2008). *The media were American: U.S. mass media in decline*. New York & Oxford: Oxford University Press.

What Is Plagiarism? (n.d.). Retrieved June 4, 2009, from http://www. plagiarism.org/learning_center/what_is_plagiarism.html.

Williams, J. M. (2007) *Style: Lessons in clarity and grace* (9th ed.). New York: Pearson Longman.

CHAPTER 4

Strategies for Success

Writing a successful media paper or professional report is much easier with a plan or strategy. This chapter covers the nuts and bolts of writing the research paper and professional report. It begins with a discussion of how to select a topic or how to work with an assigned topic, followed by suggestions for formulating a research question. Special attention is given to the process of locating, categorizing, and evaluating a wide range of sources. Readers will also find information, tips, and specific examples of how to engage in brainstorming, write an effective thesis statement, and produce an outline. The key point is to have a plan that is broken down into steps that will eventually lead to the finished paper.

OVERVIEW OF THE RESEARCH AND WRITING PROCESS

A writer's initial work on a research paper can be broken down into several steps. First, a topic is selected or assigned. As previously noted, most professors give students a choice of topics so long as the selected topic remains within the parameters of the theme for the class. For example, in a class on media technologies, topics from the telegraph to TiVo would qualify. A paper on the muckraking journalist Ida Tarbell (1857–1944) would probably *not* be acceptable in a media technologies course. With respect to writing and researching a report for work, most supervisors require and expect that a report be prepared on a particular topic. In other words, there is usually little leeway in work-related assignments. In one way, this is a relief for the writer since he or she is spared the worry associated with having to find a topic.

Second, a research question, which guides the research, is formulated. At the early stage of the writing project, both the topic and research question may be general and even somewhat vague. As research progresses, the writer should move from a general idea toward a more narrow and well-defined topic.

The next step is research. Research consists of consulting books, journal articles, documents, artifacts, and experts in order to collect information or data. A document may be testimony on some aspect of the media delivered before Congress or a policy set by the Federal Communications Commission. Depending on the topic, artifacts may include an old wooden printing press or a newly released film or CD. When consulting books and journal articles, writers will increase their chances of getting quality information by relying on sources written by experts. Experts are people who are recognized by a community of scholars as persons who can be trusted to provide reliable information. Persons who have written books published by university presses and/or articles in academic journals, and who are associated with a university or other institutions of higher learning have the credentials to be considered experts.

Research is followed by the writing of the paper or report. Whether writing for a professor, supervisor, or academic journal, a writer must follow established guidelines. These guidelines are agreed-upon rules that make it easier to read and understand the paper or report. Revisions follow the writing phase. Before the final version of the paper or report is turned in, a writer should allocate enough time to proofread and revise the paper. Because even the best writers make mistakes, it is a good idea to find someone who can read the paper without bias or fear of offending the writer. A good proofreader is someone who can point out errors in style, spelling, grammar, and punctuation, as well as raise questions about the content of the paper. These people are rare; therefore, it is usually best to have two (or three) persons read the paper. One may read for style, spelling, and grammar; another for content.

The writing process as presented herein may appear to be neat and orderly. However, it is important to remember that the process of researching and writing about the media is never straightforward. This is because writing and research about the media cannot be reduced to a cookie-cutter activity. Many writers, after investing time and effort in research, go back and revise their original research question. This can frustrate some novice writers who start their writing project with the expectation that it will only move forward. In fact, writing is a process that can be described as taking two steps forward and one step back.

RESEARCHING A TOPIC

For those who do not have an assigned topic, the first step is to find one. Start with a broad topic, as it is typically easier to narrow down a topic than to expand one. Later there will be time to narrow the topic to make it more manageable for a 10- to 15-page research paper.

To find an appropriate topic for a class-related research paper, start by getting familiar with the theme of the class. On the first day of class, listen closely to how the professor defines the focus of the class and the issues that will be covered during the semester. The focus of the class and the issues to be discussed are the parameters within which one should find a topic for the research paper. Study the class syllabus carefully because the outlined topics for lectures and discussion can also serve as broad research topics. In addition to the list of topics and lectures, the required and recommended literature can provide a general introduction to a range of possible research topics for a final paper.

For example, suppose that one is enrolled in a class titled Organizational Communication and New Media. More than likely, on the first day of class the professor will explain what she or he means by *organizations* as well as *new media*. Organizations can be both private, for-profit corporations as well as public, nonprofit companies. Examples of for-profit corporations are some insurance companies, manufacturing companies, and software development companies. Nonprofit companies might include organizations that help young people stay out of trouble by providing them with positive, structured activities, or organizations that offer the homeless meals and a place to stay. However, one needs to be cautious. Not all nonprofit companies are service oriented. Some citizens' groups are nonprofit organizations, but their focus is on providing information, not services.

In addition, there are also religious organizations and government organizations. Churches are religious organizations, but the U.S. Department of Defense is a government organization. Will all of these types of organizations be covered in the class on organizational communication and new media? If not, which will be included and which will be excluded? If nonprofit organizations will be excluded, the student would not want to write a paper on how the United Way uses e-mail to communicate with its employees. If religious organizations will not be discussed in the class, a paper on communication among members of a Christian church, Jewish synagogue, or Muslim mosque will not be considered appropriate.

Additionally, listen to how the professor defines new media. The latest technologies, such as iPods, may be considered new media. What about BlackBerries, television, or radio? Some professors might define new media as those media that made their appearance after the 1900s. Others may select a later date. Still others may take a very broad definition of new media. At one university, a professor who taught a class on new media claimed that because all media were at one time new, all media could be studied as new media. Thus it is important to know how the professor defines the topic of the class in order to select a research topic within the limits of that definition.

The following checklist can help guide the media writer through the initial stages of writing a media paper. (If the topic for the paper is preselected by the professor or supervisor, go to Step 3.)

1. Understand the parameters of the course for which the paper is being written. Attend the first day of class, read the syllabus, review the textbook(s), and pay attention to what the professor says about what the course covers as well as what it does not cover. Ask questions if any of the information is not clear.
2. Select a broad topic.
3. Begin to formulate a research question.

4. Start preliminary research by reading encyclopedia articles, relevant chapters in handbooks, reports, and some scholarly books and academic journal articles.

In sum, selecting the topic to be covered in the media research paper or professional report starts with knowledge of the parameters of media studies and the parameters of the class or assignment given by a professor or supervisor. As outlined in Chapter 2, the field of media studies is wide open. The breadth of media studies makes a variety of topics available to the media writer. Limits on the topic are created by the parameters of the course and restrictions introduced by the professor or supervisor.

RESOURCES FOR TOPIC SEARCH

Having information about the expectations for the paper can help kick-start some initial thinking about a topic. Writers are often surprised how often they will come across information they can use in their papers, essays, or reports once they have selected a topic. This phenomenon is known as *selective perception*. Selective perception refers to how people filter the information that is all around them. It is the reason why hungry people are more likely to notice ads for restaurants. When people want or need something in particular, they tend to notice information that can help satisfy their desires or meet their needs.

The phenomenon of selective perception also operates when writers are engaged in research. When a research topic is selected, and later, when writers begin to do research, their perceptual filters begin to zero in on items in magazines, newspapers, textbooks, or academic journals that may be related to the topic of interest. This is why it is important to start researching a topic early. Equally as important as starting early is starting a research project by choosing a broad topic that allows for casting a wide net to ensure that important material will not be overlooked. Later the topic can be narrowed to a manageable size.

DEFINITIONS AS RESOURCES

Many beginning media writers often overlook some of the most obvious sources for finding a topic. Textbooks, recommended books, journal articles, and other material one comes across when reading for a class can provide ideas for research papers and reports. When starting a writing project, pay attention to the terms and definitions used in the course textbook and assigned readings. Similarly, media professionals who have already been assigned a topic should start by skimming handbooks and reading encyclopedia articles and reports to become familiar with the key concepts in the relevant area of study.

Terms and their definitions can encompass the subject of the entire book or one of its chapters or sections. The definitions for the topic of a course are usually found at the beginning of the first chapter of the textbook. For example, in Jamieson and Campbell's (2006) *The Interplay of Influence*, a textbook used primarily in courses about the relationship between media and society, the authors define the topic of the book as being "about the influence of the mass media, specifically television, radio, newspapers, magazines, and the Internet" (p. 1). For a class using *The Interplay of Influence*, papers on how television news or commercials, talk radio programs or songs, editorials or sports stories, and politicians' blogs or Web sites influence people and society would all be fair game. Therefore, research papers about television sitcoms, radio commercials, newspaper stories, magazine covers, YouTube videos, RSS feeds, and Twitter messages would all be appropriate for such a class.

McNair (1995) defines *political communication* as "not only verbal or written statements, but visual means of signification such as dress, make-up, hairstyle, and logo design, i.e., all those elements of communication which might be said to constitute a political 'image' or identity" (p. 4). A paper for a class on political communication that uses McNair's book could be about speeches, press releases, or policy statements. It could also be about television ads, videos about a candidate or an issue, photos, a candidate's wardrobe, the haircut he or she prefers, and the visual symbols that represent a political party, such as an image of an elephant or a donkey. Jamieson and Campbell (2006) define *hard news* as "the report of an event that happened or that was disclosed within the previous twenty-four hours and treats an issue of ongoing concern" (p. 41). Brooks et al. (1999)

define hard news as reports about government or business. According to these researchers, reports about such events as car accidents, murders, a bank holdup, or a speech by a leader in the community are also hard news. Similar to Jamieson and Campbell, Brooks et al. believe that timeliness is a significant factor in the definition of hard news (p. 558). Thus, a paper on hard news stories on network television should not focus on stories that profile a retired public servant or someone who has been continuously working to better the community. Such stories are usually classified as feature stories, or "soft news," the type of stories that can air anytime. Instead, if the topic is hard news, the focus should be on those television news stories that, if not produced and aired immediately, lose their appeal because they quickly become "old news."

TEXTBOOKS AS RESOURCES

Course textbooks are another excellent resource for selecting a general topic for a research paper. The preface and introductory chapter in textbooks offer an overview of the material covered in subsequent chapters. Writers should pay attention to the headings of the sections in the chapters. Many textbooks include a detailed table of contents, which makes it easy to get a feel for the scope of the material covered. Within the text itself, charts and graphs, conclusions and summaries of chapters, as well as sidebars—the boxes on the side of the page that contain detailed information on a topic covered on that particular page—offer many key points, facts, and case studies that can help generate ideas for a research topic.

GLOSSARY

A glossary provides definitions for the terms used in a textbook. Glossaries can be useful resources when searching for a topic that falls within the parameters of the class. Familiarizing oneself with the terms and definitions in the glossary is important because it helps bring thinking about a topic into focus. Students will often know about or think about something without realizing that it has a name. For example, journalism students who have worked on the campus newspaper sometimes say that, while they have written descriptions to accompany photos that are printed in the newspaper, they were not aware that such descriptions are called *cutlines*. In the glossary of Harrower's (2002) *The Newspaper Designer's Handbook*, the definition of a cutline is, "A line or block of type providing descriptive information about a photo" (p. 254). With this definition as a starting point for research, a paper comparing cutlines in modern newspapers to cutlines in old newspapers could reveal differences in the writing styles of newspaper photo editors working in different eras and how these differences speak to the changing values, beliefs, and ideas of a particular community. Another research paper could examine the origin and development of cutlines. Have cutlines always accompanied photographs? If not, when were they added, and why were they first used? Have they changed over the years? If yes, what are some of the reasons that they changed? If they have not changed, how can this resistance to change be explained?

Of course, some terms or concepts are harder to define than others. The word *culture* (see Chapter 2) is one such term. There may be several, some contradictory, definitions of *culture*. In such cases, providing three or four references for those divergent definitions is important because it demonstrates the writer's awareness of the different understanding of a term by different experts in the field. In other words, it shows that the writer has done his or her research. By learning the vocabulary, or jargon, of the field, one is able to communicate with media professionals.

Relying on the glossaries listed in the required and recommended books while in search of a topic for a research paper makes it almost certain that an appropriate topic will be selected. However, as stated earlier, it is advisable to check with the professor of the class to be certain that the topic selected is one that she or he approves.

REFERENCES, BIBLIOGRAPHIES, WORKS CITED

Another important resource found near the end of a textbook is a list of references. The references can be an invaluable source of information because they can be used to track down other sources that can deepen one's understanding of a topic. While reading through the textbook, pay attention to the citations—they can be very helpful when researching a topic for a paper or report. A well-researched book, academic paper, or report will contain high-quality references (see Chapter 3). Those quality references, in turn, will contain references to other related works that can help narrow the topic, as well as broaden one's grasp of the topic of a research paper.

The important point to keep in mind is that a proper citation will always contain enough information for the reader to find the book or article being cited. Familiarization with what has been written about the topic helps avoid the mistake of making a statement or reporting a finding and claiming originality only to find that the statement or finding has been reported before. This is also a way of paying respect to those who have previously worked on, or are currently working on, the topic and have made significant contributions to our understanding of the topic. These are scholars who are interested in the same topic(s) that interests the writer. Ignoring what these researchers have reported is a sign of arrogance or of poor research practices. It is best to show respect and to learn from those who have come before.

BRAINSTORMING

Along with the idea-generating strategies mentioned previously, brainstorming is also a productive exercise. It is a quick way to come up with several topics, themes, or subjects. It can be very useful if writers become familiar with the textbook, syllabus, and basic concepts of the course before launching the brainstorming exercise. As the term implies, during a brainstorming session, ideas should fly into the conscious mind as if blown in by a storm. A key component of a brainstorming session is that any judgment on the ideas produced is put on hold. In other words, there are no bad ideas during a brainstorming session. The reason for withholding judgment is to encourage the free flow of ideas.

Begin a brainstorming session with a term or phrase. For example, take the term *print*. Write down or type all of the associations that come to mind when thinking of the word *print*. Following is a sample list of the associations that may come to mind during a brainstorming session that starts with the term *print*.

Newspapers	Printing presses
Magazines	Sports
Books	Entertainment
Machines (printing presses)	Metro
Electronic newspapers	Weekly or suburban newspapers
Reporters	Pulitzer prizes
Advertising	Fonts
Comics	Computer programs: QuarkXpress,
Typewriters	InDesign
Keyboard	Convergence

This sample list can yield ideas that can be developed into research topics. For example, take the first term in the list, *newspapers*, and explore it in more detail:

History of newspapers
Newspapers today
People who influenced the development of newspapers
Ethnic newspapers (today, history of)
Recent changes in the newspaper business
Reporters' role in news production
Sources
Salaries/benefits/profits
Great newspaper reporters
Scandals (Janet Cooke, Stephen Glass, Patricia Smith, Jayson Blair, Mike Barnicle, Jack Kelly)
Ethics
Photos
Cartoons
Political cartoons

As this example demonstrates, brainstorming is a powerful tool for generating ideas for a research paper. True, most of the ideas will be discarded, but at least one of them should show potential for being kept and developed into a research project. If not, the best part of a brainstorming session is that it can be repeated. In fact, writers are encouraged to do several brainstorming sessions using different words or terms before selecting the topic that seems the most promising for a research paper.

For instance, one of the topics generated in the sample brainstorming exercise is "scandals." Recent scandals in newspaper and magazine reporting, for example, would make a good topic either in a journalism, media ethics, or mass communication class. How was Jayson Blair able to fool so many editors at the *New York Times* for so long? A young, promising reporter, Jayson Blair, fabricated news stories based on reports he watched on CNN or read in newspapers and magazines. Then he wrote stories as if he had been to the scene and had interviewed eyewitnesses. Because he filed his stories online, no one suspected that he had never left his apartment in Brooklyn. This hoax went on for years (Mnookin, 2004). How was this possible? An answer to this question would make an interesting research paper. Considering how little time it takes to generate a long list of potential topics and ideas, it is not surprising that brainstorming is one of the best ways to start selecting a topic for a research paper.

SELECTING A TOPIC

Once the theme or focus of the course is understood, the textbook has been reviewed, and at least one brainstorming session has been conducted, it is time to select a research topic. A common mistake that too many students make is selecting a topic without giving it much consideration. As the semester progresses, they find that their topic is not as interesting as they had originally expected. Selecting another topic and starting anew means that work on the new topic will have to be intensified if the deadline is to be met. While some writers will have to change their topics, it is best to try and avoid such a problem by engaging in preliminary research and giving the decision on a topic some thought, effort, and time. Once again, the key to avoiding problems in this area is to start early. If the topic has to be changed, there will still be enough time to dedicate to researching and writing about the new topic.

Do not be too eager to change topics. Before deciding to abandon the original topic, try tweaking it. For example, the history of print is too broad of a topic. Instead of changing to another topic, focus on print in one historical time period. Select the printing press and its effect on political movements during the Renaissance, for example. Another topic might be the life of Gutenberg and what led him to the invention of the printing press. The use of satellite technology to transmit information across the country to produce a national newspaper, such as *USA Today,* would be another topic on one specific aspect of the history of print, and so would be the rise of online news sources like *Slate* or the *Huffington Post.*

Another problem related to selecting a topic is the lack of material available to research the topic adequately. This may be an indication that the topic is too narrow. Perhaps the topic needs to be broadened or the time period covered in the paper expanded. The opposite problem, an overabundance of sources, usually indicates that the topic is too broad. In this case, the writer should try narrowing the topic or time period covered (see previous discussion).

Keep in mind that these kinds of problems can usually be minimized or even avoided altogether by investing time in preliminary research. When selecting a topic, use what is gleaned from preliminary research—such as skimming books and reading journal articles—to guide the selection of a topic. Pay attention to how previous researchers limited their topics. They usually do so for a reason, such as the number of words they are allotted or the time available to write the paper. If a media writer has to cover a topic in four or five thousand words, or 10 to 15 pages, and only has one semester to write the paper, some broad topics, such as the history of popular music, are out of the question. It is more likely that a topic such as the influence of YouTube on the popularity of singer Susan Boyle, a contestant on the television show *Britain's Got Talent,* would be more manageable.

If there is an option of choosing a topic for a paper, writers are encouraged to find something of interest, something that arouses curiosity. Many important discoveries started with being curious. Curiosity, research, and discovery are inextricably linked.

Being curious about the world can lead to many research questions related to media. Why are some movies popular while others flop? Why do some people buy books while others prefer to download and read them on Kindle? Do people who buy CDs later download the music they buy onto their iPods? If so, what distinguishes such people from those who prefer to listen to the CD on a home entertainment center? What do different people listen to on their iPods: music, audiobooks, motivational speeches, religious readings, or podcasts of missed radio programs? What accounts for these differences? These are examples of how curiosity can lead to research questions. (Chapter 5 offers several examples of how writers can use curiosity and imagination to find a topic for a paper and formulate a research question.)

FORMULATING A TENTATIVE RESEARCH QUESTION

After selecting a general topic for the research paper, the next step is developing a tentative research question. At this stage, the purpose of developing such a question is to narrow the research topic further. As noted before, a mistake many beginning writers make is selecting a topic that is too broad to be adequately covered in a 10- to 15-page paper or report. When writing about the media, a rule of thumb to keep in mind is that the more specific the topic, the better it will be covered in a research paper or report.

Some students believe that by selecting a broad topic they demonstrate a breadth of knowledge. However, professors are usually more interested in a thorough examination of a narrow topic rather than a cursory overview of a broad subject. Occasionally, a student will propose to write a paper on a topic such as the development of writing from clay tablets in ancient Sumeria to the fax machine. Most professors would not be impressed with such a broad topic because, as experts on media topics themselves, they are quite aware that it is impossible to cover so much territory in one paper. Many academics have spent their entire professional careers studying only a handful of topics, sometimes very narrowly defined topics, in depth. This is what defines them as experts. Therefore, it would be difficult for someone who has spent a career focusing his or her research efforts on political cartoons in U.S. magazines of the 1800s to trust that a student can cover thousands of years of the history of the media in one semester. Even a seemingly narrow topic, such as the representation of African Americans on television, would be too broad. It would be better, for instance, to narrow the topic to the representation of African American men on primetime television in the 1950s, a time when few African American males appeared on television. Another possibility would be to narrow the topic by focusing on African American women in police dramas that aired in prime time in the 1990s.

Media professionals may have the opposite problem. While students are often asked by their professors to narrow their research topic, media professionals may be asked by their supervisors to cover a topic that is too broad for a professional report. Too often the supervisor is trying to get more bang for the buck, so to speak. In these situations, it is important not to promise more than can be delivered. Take time to explain to the supervisor why writing a comprehensive history of public relations is not possible. Such a project would take years to complete.

While the topic selection frames the research interests of the writer, the research question gives the paper a purpose. Similar to the selection of a topic, the development of a research question moves from the general to the specific. It is always a good idea to ask *who*, *what*, *when*, and *where*, and answer these questions in a research paper or professional report.

For example, to explore the early days of television, a writer may start by asking the following questions:

Who invented electronic television?
What was the first sport transmitted over television?
When was the first television broadcast made?
Where was the first television station built?

These questions can all be answered by looking up the factual information (name, sport, date, or location) in an encyclopedia, history, or reference book. While these questions are undoubtedly important, a researcher should come up with a research question that asks *how* and/or *why* because such questions prompt a critical assessment of the topic (Booth, Colomb, & Williams, 2008, p. 41).

In some instances, a question that begins with *what* can also be a powerful research tool. Notice how the focus of a research topic changes when a *how*, *why*, or *what* question is asked. How did print influence culture? How did print influence Western European culture in the 1500s? Why did the printing press spread throughout Europe so quickly? What were the effects of print on business practices during the Renaissance? What was the relationship between the business of printing and European monarchies during the Renaissance? The research questions that start with *how*, *why*, or *what* give the research project focus. Once a preliminary research question is formulated, the next step is to find out what has been published on the topic.

After the following section on preliminary research as an essential step in formulating a good research question, the challenge of coming up with a successful research question is reintroduced and several examples are provided.

THE ROLE OF PRELIMINARY RESEARCH IN RESHAPING A TENTATIVE MEDIA RESEARCH QUESTION

Preliminary research is an important step in formulating a research question. It takes prior research and some background knowledge to construct a question that will guide the research project. Moreover, the knowledge acquired during such preliminary work will undoubtedly be helpful in the writing phase of the project. The question many students and media professionals ask is, "Where and how do I start my preliminary research?" Following are some answers to this question.

ENCYCLOPEDIAS

Start your research and the further development of a tentative research question by reviewing encyclopedias, such as the *Museum of Broadcast Communications Encyclopedia of Television* (Horace Newcomb, ed.), the *Museum of Broadcast Communications Encyclopedia of Radio* (Christopher H. Sterling, ed.), the *International Encyclopedia of Communication* (Wolfgang Donsbach, ed.), the *Film Encyclopedia* (Ephraim Katz, ed.), and the *Encyclopedia of*

Hollywood (Scott Siegel and Barbara Siegel). There is also an *Encyclopedia of Media and Politics* (Todd M. Schaefer and Thomas A. Birkland, eds.) and the *Encyclopedia of Journalism* (Christopher H. Sterling, general ed.). If researching a person in media, do not overlook sources such as the various encyclopedias of women; the *Encyclopedia Latina: History, Culture and Society in the United States* (Ilan Stavans, ed.); the *Oxford Encyclopedia of Latinos and Latinas in the United States* (Suzanne Oboler and Deena J. Gonzales, eds.); *Africana: The Encyclopedia of the African and African American Experience* (Henry Louis Gates and Kwame Anthony Appiah, eds.). Encyclopedias are excellent sources for getting started on a research project because they provide an overview of a topic or person, as well as key words and references that can be used later for further research.

Encyclopedia entries also provide the name(s) of the author(s) of the entry and a list of the author's sources. There is a good chance that the person who wrote the encyclopedia entry has written other articles on the subject, and maybe even a book or two. Take notice of the sources the author of the encyclopedia article cites. These sources are invaluable to a researcher. In your research journal, make a note of the article, its main point or focus, and the sources listed. Also note any terms and definitions used in an encyclopedia article.

For example, suppose the research topic is the colorization of black-and-white movies. In the *Encyclopedia of Television*, Gary Burns (2004) defines *colorization* as "a computerized process that adds color to a black-and-white movie or TV program" (p. 556). Burns also provides information on the moral arguments against colorization, as well as arguments in support of colorization. Finally, he provides the sources he used to write his encyclopedia entry that include several journal articles and government documents.

Thus, in addition to the definition of the term *colorization* and a brief overview of the debates surrounding the issue, Burns also provides sources that can be useful in further research on several challenging issues behind the colorization debates that took place in the late 1980s. This example of looking up *colorization* in the *Encyclopedia of Television* demonstrates how valuable encyclopedia articles can be in finding definitions, debates about a topic, and sources.

Keep in mind, however, that while encyclopedias are good sources for starting research, they are considered a poor substitute for scholarly journals and academic books and, therefore, should not be the only type of sources used. The reason for this is that encyclopedia articles are usually brief accounts about a topic. Most encyclopedia articles barely begin to scratch the surface of a research topic; they usually do not and cannot include all the nuances or details about a topic in a single entry. Typically, publishers of encyclopedias emphasize breadth rather than depth of knowledge. For this reason, encyclopedias are excellent sources for getting started on a research project, but they are not suitable sources for in-depth research.

Writing Tip: Use encyclopedias during the very early stages of a research project to gain quick access to information and sources about a topic.

ELECTRONIC DATABASES

After reading several encyclopedia articles and making notes about the author(s) of the articles, as well as those cited, log on to a university library's Web site and examine several available databases such as LexisNexis, EbscoHost, JSTOR, and ERIC. These and other databases allow access to the full text of numerous scholarly journals and other academic publications. Depending on the topic, it may also be beneficial to take a look at what trade magazines, such as *Broadcasting and Cable*, *Wired*, *Advertising Age*, *Columbia Journalism Review*, *Quill*, and others, have reported about the topic. Pay attention to any controversies or debates that recur, and note them in the research journal. Note also the recurrence of any names. Persons who are interviewed repeatedly about a topic, who write articles themselves, or are referred to in articles, tend to be considered experts on that topic. Make a note of those persons, the topic(s), and the university, government agency, or research institute with which they are affiliated, and use the information to track down their work.

A *warning about Web sites*

While Web sites maintained by a college or university library can usually be trusted, not everything found on the Internet is suitable for inclusion in a research paper. In fact, most of what is on the Internet would not be considered an appropriate or reliable source by a professor or supervisor. When engaged in research, *always* question the legitimacy of Web sites. The reason for getting into this habit is that many Web sites are created and maintained by persons or organizations that are promoting a cause. This, in and of itself, is not a problem. Many individuals and groups have Web sites that provide valuable information about the media. However, when doing scholarly research on the media, it is imperative that only information from reliable sources is accessed and used. What follows describes a few Web sites that can provide trustworthy and updated information for media-related research.

When looking for the number of television and radio stations in operation in the United States, the Federal Communications Commission (FCC) Web site can be trusted to provide such information (http://www.fcc.gov). In addition, the FCC offers other information related to media in the United States. For example, its Web site has not only information about the FCC, its duties, and responsibilities, but also statistical reports, information about telecommunications service in rural America, and a brief history of communication in the United States, including a short history of the Internet. One of the FCC reports provides information about complaints to the FCC.

Another source for information about mass media is the National Association of Broadcasters (NAB) (http://www.nab.org). From its Web site, a writer can learn about positions taken by the NAB on a variety of topics, such as the FCC's requirement that stations keep recordings of their programming in order to allow the FCC access to the programming to enforce regulations about indecency and profanity (http://www.nab.org/AM/Template.cfm?Section=Resources & Template=/CM/HTMLDisplay.cfm&ContentID=7402).

However, it should be pointed out that such information may not be objective. The NAB's role is to represent the nation's broadcasters. In fact, it does not pretend to be objective. For this reason, while the information the organization provides may be useful, it is important to seek opposing views to gain a balanced understanding of a topic or issue. For example, the NAB Web site argues against "unreasonable restrictions" on media ownership and would like to see the FCC lift such restrictions. Other organizations, Free Press, for example (http://www.freepress.net/media_issues/consolidation), argue against media consolidation and for more diversity of ownership of media. It would be unusual for the NAB to argue against the interests of its members. Accordingly, it would also be odd if Free Press began to promote "Big Media." This is why it is important to search for and include alternative perspectives in one's research.

Questioning a Web site begins by learning who is responsible for its information. When coming across any information on a Web site, get into the habit of clicking on the "About us" page. This page should reveal the name of the organization that maintains the Web site and provide the name or names of individuals associated with the Web site and the e-mail address of the organization's Webmaster. Beware of Web sites that do not list the names or e-mails of persons responsible for the Web site. Also, check the date when the Web site was last updated. Another clue that should give a reason for concern is if e-mail inquiries to a Web site are not answered. Ignoring legitimate questions is a worrisome sign that should leave the researcher to wonder why the organization that maintains the Web site is not responding.

Review a particular Web site by looking at its Uniform Resource Locator, or URL, paying particular attention to the last portion of the Web address. For instance, the American Society of Newspaper Editors, also known as ASNE, has the Web address http://www .asne.org. The URL tag "org" reveals that ASNE is a nonprofit organization, and that it uses its Web site to explain and promote its policies, activities, and goals. If the URL ends in "gov," that Web page is maintained by a government agency. An educational institution will have "edu" as part of its Web address. The tag "com" stands for "commercial entity" and indicates that a private company or business is behind the Web site. Individuals can have Web sites that represent them either as private persons or as members of a particular organization, university, or other group. It is not always easy to distinguish between the two because many personal Web sites are often embedded into larger domains or contain links to such domains.

Writing Tip: It is worth pointing out that many university libraries provide help with demystifying Web sites by showing how to decode the URL information, in addition to providing other helpful information about an Internet search. For instance, the Sheridan Libraries Web site, Johns Hopkins University, maintains the Understanding and Decoding URLs page (http://www.library.jhu.edu/researchhelp/general/evaluating/url.html) as part of their guide for evaluating information found on the Internet. Numerous libraries offer interactive presentations and tutorials that help their patrons navigate through the strengths and weaknesses of Web searching. The University of Michigan Library's Searchpath tutorial (http://www.lib.umich.edu/ugl/searchpath/) is one such tool. Apparently, Searchpath has been very effective because a number of university libraries provide a link to Searchpath on their Web sites.

Another important aspect to keep in mind when using Web sites is being aware that there exists a multitude of opinions and value judgments on the same subject. For example, a Web site about children's television programs that is maintained by television broadcasters will have information that is different from a Web site maintained by parents who are concerned about the content of children's television programs. As noted earlier, when doing research, including an online investigation, be sure to locate at least one or two sources that provide opposing views to the ones already found. Multiple viewpoints help sharpen the arguments of a paper and should not be ignored.

CATEGORIZING SOURCES

In order to identify reliable and relevant sources for a particular research project, a writer should also be familiar with their categorization. Sources can be categorized as primary, secondary, or tertiary. A primary source is a document written by someone who had or has firsthand experience or evidence regarding some person(s) or event(s). A recorded interview with someone who participated in some event or activity, such as a film director who worked on a movie, would be considered a primary source. Newspapers are a primary source used by media historians to study the past. If a research project is about films depicting the Old West, then Westerns, such as *The Oxbow Incident* (Wellman, 1943), *The Searchers* (Ford, 1956),

The Good, the Bad and the Ugly (Leone, 1966), and *3:10 to Yuma* (Mangold, 2007) would all qualify as primary sources. Primary sources contain the information, or "raw data," about a topic that the researcher is studying and writing about (Booth et al., 2008, p. 69). It is important to note that copies of original sources in different formats or media—microfilm, microfiche, or a digital version—are still considered primary sources because their content, not their original format, classifies them as primary sources. For example, when writing about freedom of the press, the First Amendment of the Constitution would be considered a primary source, regardless of whether one is reading the original Constitution or a copy. (For further discussion on primary sources and the variety of their representations, see the Yale University Web site: http://www.yale.edu/ collections_collaborative/primarysources/primarysources.html.)

Secondary sources consist of books or articles based on primary sources. They contain the views, ideas, and/or opinions of the researcher who collected and analyzed the information from primary sources. Briefly, a secondary source can be understood as analysis or interpretation of primary sources. For example, if a researcher publishes a book about Westerns, such a book would be a secondary source with respect to the movies themselves. Well-researched books and articles about Westerns can be cited to either back up or critique the arguments in a research paper that focuses on this genre.

In addition to primary and secondary sources, there are also tertiary sources. Tertiary sources are reports based on secondary sources. They are usually a composite of research that has been done in some area of study. Because of their summative nature, tertiary sources are often viewed as generalizations. This is not necessarily a bad thing. Summaries can be very helpful, especially in the beginning of the research project. The problem is that in the process of generalizing, data tend to be somewhat simplified and, in some cases, omitted. For this reason, tertiary sources are often considered the least useful for research purposes. However, least useful does not mean "useless."

The strength of tertiary sources is their usefulness in getting a research project started. Tertiary sources, such as encyclopedias, can provide a quick overview of a topic and a list of helpful references. In general, however, researchers should try to avoid citing too many tertiary sources in a research paper or professional report and, instead, build their argument using mostly primary and secondary sources. If a specific work mentioned in a tertiary source is relevant to the research topic, a writer should find and analyze that work rather than rely on the tertiary source's summary.

Writing Tip: It is important to make an effort to move away from the idea of "good" and "bad" sources. Whether a source is good or bad depends on the topic of research and the research question. Rather than think in absolute terms, it is better to remain flexible and to think in terms of how best to answer one's research question.

Learning to identify and categorize sources is an important step in writing about the media. It can make the writer more flexible and at the same time more careful when working with various sources. It can also help the writer focus his or her efforts when answering a research question. An important component of managing sources is knowing which of them can be trusted (see Chapter 3).

WORKING WITH SOURCES

While writers should not ignore popular books and magazines, these publications should not become the only sources of information. Instead, as mentioned in Chapter 3, writers should rely mostly on academic books, scholarly journal articles, and legitimate Web sites. Academic or scholarly sources are written by respected academics or media professionals who have distinguished themselves as thoughtful observers and analysts of the trends in the field of media studies. The same standards also apply to articles that have appeared in peer-reviewed journals that are sponsored by national professional organizations, such as the National Communication Association (NCA), the International Communication Association (ICA), the Association for Education in Journalism and Mass Communication (AEJMC), the International Association for Media and Communication Research (IAMCR), and the Broadcast Educators Association (BEA). Some scholarly organizations are regional, such as the Western Communication Association (WSCA) and the Eastern

Communication Association (ECA). In addition to the publications sponsored by the organizations mentioned above, many universities or media/communication programs publish journals. For example, the Communication Department at the University of Iowa edits the *Journal of Communication Inquiry*; the John H. Johnson School of Communications at Howard University hosts the *Howard Journal of Communications*. The University of Wisconsin at Madison and the University of Texas at Austin provide the editorial support for the *Velvet Light Trap*. With so many high-quality scholarly publications available to them, writers are bound to find a number of relevant and reliable sources. The next step involves thorough work with the located sources.

READING CRITICALLY

Many students who begin reading books written by academics and articles published in scholarly journals find them challenging. This is because the average reader's daily diet of reading material consists of newspapers, magazines, and Web sites that target the general population. Typically, the reading level required to understand a newspaper story or magazine article is anywhere from 8th grade to 12th grade. In contrast, academic journal articles and books require a college reading level. Consequently, reading academic publications requires more time and concentration than does reading newspaper or magazine articles. The articles in newspapers and magazines, while they may have valuable information, do not make much of a demand on the reading or critical thinking skills of their audience. This is why newspapers and magazines can be read while riding the bus or subway, eating lunch, listening to music, or watching TV.

Journal articles, on the other hand, can be difficult to read and comprehend. Like much college-level reading, journal articles require close attention. They should be read carefully, noting main ideas and writing questions and comments in the research journal (see Chapter 3 for more information about keeping a research journal). This is active, critical reading. When reading a journal article, start with the abstract, which usually consists of from 75 to 250 words. The abstract is a summary of the main ideas developed in the article. It provides key words and phrases either in the text or in a separate line. These key words are important because they can be used to conduct more focused searches on a university's database.

The introduction to the article should explain what issue, topic, or research question is being addressed. Questions to ask while reading the introduction are: What is the writer trying to explain? What is new about the explanation? Why is the explanation important? How does it differ from previous explanations? A good introduction should offer answers to all these questions. The introduction should also provide an overview of the points that will be explored, as well as a general outline that the essay will follow.

The next sections of the article consist of elaborations of the points mentioned in the introduction. These are usually addressed in the order in which they were presented in the introduction. It is customary to follow the introduction with a literature review, which presents a summary of published works relevant to the media topic at hand. Recall the point made earlier about writers joining a conversation with their readers. By reviewing prior research on the topic of the paper or chapter, the writer demonstrates that he or she is familiar with what has been discussed about the topic in the past, as well as what is being discussed in the present. In so doing, the writer is placing his or her article in the context of previous discussions about the topic. Showing knowledge and understanding of the ideas or theories surrounding the media topic and how one's essay fits into the larger context earns the respect of readers.

Evidence is presented to support, or back up, any claims made in the introduction. One aspect of academic writing that makes it challenging to read and understand is that it tends to favor more nuanced interpretations of reality than those usually found in more conventional writing. The appeal of popular magazine and newspaper articles, as well as books for general consumption, lies in their sweeping statements and often gross categorizations of complex issues and phenomena. It is easier to find clear demarcations of "right" and "wrong" in such publications. Take the everyday discussions about popular music as an example. Typically, there are two opposing sides. On one side are those who find popular music to be detrimental to the young people who listen to and enjoy it. This side claims that popular music leads to disrespect for civic authority, the family, and other social institutions. Rarely do critics of popular music find any redeeming social qualities in it. On the other side, supporters of popular music tend to promote it wholeheartedly. This is understandable, since in an environment in which popular music is attacked, the tendency will be to "circle the wagons." Consequently, in this camp, popular music is considered great; it is society that is the problem. This side argues that popular music is just reflecting a society that is plagued by corrupt leaders, dysfunctional families, and crumbling social institutions.

In contrast to conventional arguments, academic writing about popular music tends toward more balanced or nuanced views. Yes, some aspects of popular music may be offensive, argue some academics, but at the same time such music can raise questions about problems in society and the role of the state. Popular music, like other forms of popular culture, may also express frustrations with the status quo. Rather than advocate for a ban on popular music or accept it without criticism, most scholars of popular culture call for a critical analysis of popular music to gain a better understanding of the political, economic, and social conditions in which it is produced, distributed, and consumed. Scholars of popular culture are also aware that many forms of popular music once considered offensive, such as jazz or rock 'n' roll, have become part of mainstream culture (Zolov, 1999).

Such nuanced views require more attention from the reader. Rather than gross generalizations such as "good" and "bad," academic writing has a tendency toward more subtle views of social phenomena. Thus to gain a deeper understanding of an academic work, the reader has to think critically and engage with the text. It is important to ask what the writer in an academic publication is trying to communicate. What is she or he suggesting? How is the writer balancing perspectives? Who is being cited? Are opposing views acknowledged in a respectful, yet critical, manner? These are the types of questions that the reader needs to keep in mind when critically reading a journal article or academic book.

In other words, reading critically means asking questions about the material being presented. For example, suppose a journal article reports the results of an investigation of how newspapers report stories about youth gangs. One can begin by asking a series of questions: "What is a gang?" That is, how does the writer of the article define a *gang*? Is his or her definition the same as that of other writers in the field? If not, how do the definitions differ? What reasons are given for these differences? If the writer is proposing a new definition of a gang, why does he or she reject or revise previous definitions? Do the reasons given for a new definition of a gang seem valid? Are there books or articles that deal specifically with the problem of defining a gang? In contrast to the popular notion that there is agreement among academics about the definition of terms in the field of media studies, students are often surprised to find that there is little agreement among researchers on the definitions of terms.

What, for example, is a newspaper? Is it a daily publication, such as the *Washington Post* or the *L.A. Times*? What about newspapers that are published weekly, like many alternative or suburban newspapers? Can a newspaper be published monthly, or does that make it a magazine? But many magazines are published weekly. What is the difference between a newspaper and a magazine? To muddle the waters even more, consider that many newspapers today are never published. They are posted online. Are online newspapers considered newspapers for the purposes of research? So if the topic of research is newspapers, how will online publications that deliver news and information be defined?

To complicate matters further, the United States Post Office has its own definitions of what constitutes a newspaper or periodical based on "mailability standards" (http://pe.usps.gov/text/dmm300/707.htm#wp1074538). According to the U.S. Post Office, a periodical "is one published at a stated frequency with the intent to continue publication indefinitely, with these characteristics:

1. The continuity of the periodical must show from issue to issue. Continuity is shown by serialization of articles or by successive issues carrying the same style, format, theme, or subject matter.
2. The primary purpose of the periodical must be the transmission of information.

3. The content of the periodical may consist of original or reprinted articles on one topic or many topics, listings, photographs, illustrations, graphs, a combination of advertising and nonadvertising matter, comic strips, legal notices, editorial material, cartoons, or other subject matter.

4. The primary distribution of each issue must be made before that of each succeeding issue."

Thus, as can be seen from the features listed above, the U.S. Post Office has its own reasons for defining newspapers and other periodicals, which have to do with setting the price of delivery. Such definitions do influence how newspapers and magazines are designed and distributed, as well as what content they carry and how often people will read them. These types of definitions are also important because they give researchers another perspective on what constitutes media, in this case, print media distributed via the U.S. Post Office.

Asking questions such as the previous ones, as well as seeking different definitions of media from diverse sources, can lead to questions for further research. A good research process inevitably involves locating pertinent academic sources. At the initial stages of doing research, the number of sources found on a particular topic may seem overwhelming. With the abundance of sources on media topics, the writer has to be able to assess such sources rather efficiently. Following are tips on how to "sift through" typical academic sources, books and journal articles, in order to identify the ones that are most relevant to the selected research topic.

IDENTIFYING RELEVANT SOURCES

Start reading a scholarly book by going over the table of contents. Get a feel for the contents of the book by reading the chapter titles and asking how the chapters relate to one another. Read the introductory and last chapters quickly. If it appears from this quick reading that the book may contain useful information with respect to the research question or topic selected, read the introduction more closely. Continue with the rest of the book. Remember to make notes in the research journal while reading.

When reading a journal article, always start with the abstract, then read the introduction to the article to get more details of what the article covers. Next, read the conclusion. If the article appears promising, that is, its abstract, introduction, and conclusion seem relevant to the topic being researched, then carefully read the entire article.

Learning how to read and evaluate academic sources may take some time, but it is worth the investment. It will give writers confidence in the statements they make in their own research papers or reports. Relying on weak sources, such as popular magazines and books, will cast a shadow of doubt over the validity of a research project. In contrast, referring to academic books, scholarly journal articles, and legitimate Web sites will ensure that the material included in a research paper has received approval from professionals who know their subject. This will make arguments in the research paper or report more convincing and situate one's work in the context of the ongoing academic conversation.

REFINING THE RESEARCH QUESTION

The next phase after preliminary research is refining one's tentative research question. There is a common misconception that writing a research paper consists of collecting and synthesizing information. This view, however, overlooks the point that a good research paper or professional report answers a research question. Answering a research question is what gives a research paper its focus. This section outlines steps for developing a research question that guides the research process and gives the research paper or report a coherent structure.

Suppose that in the course of preliminary research, a writer who is interested in investigating the development of television in America has found several articles that discuss the origins of television in the United States. Based on this preliminary research, the topic of the origins of television seems like a worthy one to pursue and develop into a research paper. The writer should start by asking the following questions. *What* are the different views on the diffusion of television in the United States? *What* are some of the reasons given for those views? *What* kinds of arguments are made to support the different views?

The answers to *what* questions can give the researcher a good idea of the material that is available for research. Once these questions have been explored, it is time to turn to the *how* and *why* questions that are the next step in formulating a manageable research question. As mentioned earlier, questions that start with *how* or *why*, as well as *what*, tend to lead to answers that offer compelling findings and analyses. Consider this *how* question: *How* did television come to dominate leisure activity in the United States in the 1950s? Such a question requires the writer to go beyond simple fact-finding and instead engage in in-depth exploration of the reasons behind the phenomenon.

Consider another example of a possible research question, a *why* question: *Why* did television come to dominate leisure activity in the United States in the 1950s? Like the previous *how* question, this question serves as a central idea around which a research paper or report can be constructed. Notice that both questions are broad enough to allow for a productive discussion of the topic, yet specific enough to narrow the scope of the research paper or report and keep the research and writing manageable.

A good research paper, like a good story, should have a point. In their seminal work on storytelling, Labov and Fanshel (1977) argue that stories that are not coherent or compelling may evoke the dreaded "So what?" question from the audience. By constructing a good research question and providing compelling evidence that answers it, a writer simultaneously anticipates and precludes the "So what?" reaction. The following is an example of how to use different types of questions (*what, how,* and *why*) in the process of exploring a topic for a research paper.

Suppose the topic of ethical decisions regarding television news is being considered as a possible research topic. The first set of *wh-* questions helps explore this area and identify a potential focus for a study.

What is meant by media ethics?
Who are the people in the newsroom making ethical decisions related to television news?
What kinds of ethical decisions do they deal with?

Where (in the newsroom, out in the field), and under what conditions, should ethical decisions be made?

These questions require that the personnel responsible for making ethical decisions about news stories be identified. They also require that some criteria be offered for different situations in which a need for ethical decision-making may arise. For instance, breaking news that must receive immediate attention versus a feature story, which can air several days later. The final question leads to a further discussion of whether ethical decisions about television news stories are the responsibility of top management, or if there might be situations when a news crew has to take responsibility for making an ethical decision. For example, if the news director is not available and there is a breaking news story, should the news crew (reporter, photographer, and satellite truck operator) make a decision to broadcast a story or should the producer of the newscast, who is at the station, make the decision?

The next set of questions adds more depth to the issue:

How should ethical decisions regarding television news be made?
Why should ethical decisions regarding television news be made?

Questions that start with *how* and *why* tend to pique the interest of readers in ways that other *wh-* questions do not. *How* and *why* questions draw the reader closer to the topic, while the other questions tend to relate facts or procedures. Both are important sets of questions, but answers to the *how* and *why* questions are the ones readers usually find most interesting.

FORMULATING AN EFFECTIVE THESIS STATEMENT

Finding answers to the research question moves research forward and helps writers formulate a working thesis for a paper. While a solid research question shapes research and narrows the topic, a thesis sentence provides a summary of the writer's contribution to the discussion of a particular issue. Every media paper, regardless of its goal and scope, must have a main idea—its thesis. Most research publications, including papers and books that explore the topic of the media, are argumentative—that is, they contain a debatable thesis supported with evidence. This means that others may disagree with the author's conclusions. In contrast to the argumentative mode of research papers and books, reference literature, such as encyclopedia articles, is usually descriptive. Namely, reference literature synthesizes prior research on a topic without making any new arguments. Writers of a media paper, unless their assignment is to summarize prior work on a topic, should be careful not to limit their papers to a compilation of prior work on the topic, but instead engage in and contribute to the "conversation" on the selected topic. In this regard, formulating an effective thesis sentence is an important step in shaping a successful media paper, because a thesis statement presents the core argument of the paper, its main claim.

In the course of research and writing, writers often revise their thesis statement to reflect the development of their initial argument. Thus, a working thesis should guide one's research and writing process without restricting it. To write an effective thesis statement, researchers should make sure that their claim is argumentative and that it contains an answer, supported by evidence, to the research question. Next are a few examples of how writers can identify and revise ineffective thesis statements. For instance, a writer who is investigating why movie theater audiences declined in the post-World War II United States proposes the following thesis: "Between 1946 and 1956, the movie theatre audience decreased by almost 50 percent, which indicates the decline of the movie industry in post-war America." Such a sentence is an ineffective thesis statement because it does not answer the research question of why during the post-war period fewer people were going to the movies. Moreover, this thesis statement simply provides the facts without argumentation. A writer can test whether his or her thesis is argumentative by completing the introductory clause "I argue that" with his or her thesis. For example, it is evident that the sentence "I argue that between 1946 and 1956 the movie theatre audience decreased by almost 50 percent, which indicates the decline of the movie industry in post-war America" does not present a viable argument, and, therefore, is an ineffective thesis statement. The writer has to revise the thesis statement, and to do so he or she may have to conduct more research.

In the process of researching the topic further, the writer learns that the improving economic situation after World War II that created inexpensive housing in the suburbs, the increasing popularity of drive-in theaters, the growing number of young families with children moving to the suburbs, and traffic congestion in downtown areas were among the reasons why movie theater audiences declined in post-war America. Taking into account these findings, the researcher then produces the following thesis statement: "Changing economic, demographic, and social factors caused the decline of Hollywood audiences in post-war America." While this statement is a solid working thesis because it answers the research question and passes the "I argue" test, it still can be improved by anticipating and acknowledging the differing views on the topic.

While investigating a topic, writers are likely to come across alternative conceptualizations and interpretations of the same events and phenomena. When they do, they should address them in the paper. To ignore alternative conceptualizations and interpretations would not only be unethical, but also strip the argument of the nuances and complexities, and as a result, make the paper weaker. Similarly, simplifying or misrepresenting the findings of other researchers who have come to different conclusions will not make the paper stronger either (see Tannen, 1998, pp. 268–269). Instead, when writers respectfully acknowledge opposing views and present their own claims clearly and with sufficient evidence, they strengthen the argument of the paper (see Booth et al., 2008). For instance, the writer who researches the reasons behind the decline of movie theatre audiences in post-war America finds that, contrary to his or her claim, many researchers believe that it was the introduction of television that caused the decline. For instance, some studies show that while in 1946 only 0.02 percent of American households owned a TV set, by 1955, more than 64 percent did (see Lev, 2006, p. 7). Many researchers used these statistics, as well as other evidence, to claim that television was the major factor behind the decline in movie theater attendance in the 1940s and 1950s.

The writer should acknowledge these claims and findings in the paper and formulate a thesis that recognizes these different understandings of the drop in movie theater attendance in post-war America. In so doing, the writer simultaneously acknowledges, responds to, and anticipates the claims of other researchers and readers.

The following is an example of a thesis statement that, along with the main claim, acknowledges a different take on the topic: "Although it is common to blame the decline of film on the rise of the new medium of television, it was a web of changing economic, demographic, and social factors that caused the decline of Hollywood audiences in post-war America." Such a statement lets a reader know that the writer is aware of the different understandings of the issue. As Booth et al. (2008, pp. 122–124) suggest, the qualifications that start with "although" or "even though" enrich the argument by making it more complex and multifaceted. Formulating an effective thesis statement helps media writers bring the seemingly disparate threads of one's research into focus, an important step in producing a successful media paper.

WORKING WITH AN OUTLINE

Another tool that shapes one's research and findings into a coherent paper is an outline. Similar to the working thesis, an outline should be treated as a helpful tool in guiding one's research and writing rather than as an added burden. In other words, an outline is designed to assist writers in organizing their work. Having an outline during the early stages of the project helps systematize one's research; in later stages, an outline helps with the logical organization of a paper. While many successful writers admit that they rarely create elaborate outlines at the onset of the writing project, most, if not all, stress that they use some type of outline or plan before they start writing. Writers should use different outlines during different stages of the writing project (Booth et al., 2008). Accordingly, a writer may start with a rough outline that simply lists the points he or she wants to make. Following is a rough outline for the paper that explores the decline of Hollywood movie audiences in post-war America:

1. Introduction (Between 1946 and 1956, movie theater audiences decreased by almost 50 percent. Why?)
2. Reason A: Spread of television
3. Reason B: Suburban living of young families: no movie theaters close by
4. Reason C: Rise of drive-ins
5. Reason D: Poor quality of movies
6. Conclusion

Such an informal outline helps the writer start building a logical argument and identify gaps in research. For instance, the writer realizes that she or he needs more evidence to support the claim that young families were moving to the suburbs, as well as to explain the reason behind this movement and its link to the decline of Hollywood audiences.

Some professors and supervisors may ask writers to turn in formal outlines before they can submit final papers. This step not only allows writers to receive feedback before the paper is finished, but it also provides an opportunity to work on the organization of the paper. If not specified, a writer should find out what type of a formal outline is expected. There are two types of formal outlines: A topic outline and a sentence outline. While a topic outline uses words, phrases, and clauses to show the hierarchical relationship between different points, a sentence outline, accordingly, uses complete sentences. Each type of formal outline has its advantages: a topic outline is more succinct and thus requires less formal writing, whereas a sentence outline takes more time to produce. On the plus side, a writer can use the sentences from the sentence outline as the elements of a paper, often as topic sentences in paragraphs. Each of the outlines helps a writer organize a media paper logically, thus making it coherent (see more information on coherence and cohesion in Chapter 5). To show the relationships between the points of the paper, both types of the formal outline can use either the number-letter or the decimal format. Again, it is best to ask the professor or supervisor, or consult the publication guidelines before committing to a particular outline format. Some software, such as the widely used Microsoft Word, has tools that can help writers format their outlines (the following sample outlines were formatted in Microsoft Word).

Writing Tip: To create an outline using Microsoft Word software, open a Microsoft Word document, click on Format, *select* Bullets and Numbering, *select* Outline Numbered, *and, finally, select the appropriate type of outline format.*

Typically, an outline, either topic or sentence, begins with a thesis statement. Following are samples of the topic and sentence outlines that use the number-letter sequence.

Sample Topic Outline

Thesis statement: Although it is common to blame the decline of film audiences on the rise of the medium of television, it was a web of changing economic, demographic, and social factors that caused the decline of Hollywood audiences in post-World War II America.

I. Introduction: A new medium as the alleged reason behind the decline of an older medium
   A. Radio as the reason for the decline of newspaper circulation
   B. Television as the cause for the drop in the movie theater attendance in post-war America
   C. The Internet as the cause of the weakening of newspaper circulation

II. Body: Reasons why Hollywood audiences declined in post-war America
   A. Booming post-war economy and the expanding buying power of American families
      1. GI Bill making low-interest loans available
      2. Young families buying houses in the suburbs
      3. America beginning its love affair with cars
      4. Mass-produced appliances becoming accessible
   B. Changing demographics and life styles of Americans
      1. People getting married at earlier ages
      2. People starting families earlier than previous generations

C. Changing economy as a factor in changing lifestyles
   1. Urban areas declining
   2. Young families living in the suburbs
   3. More families entertaining at home
   4. Drive-ins making available inexpensive suburban family entertainment

D. The declining quality of Hollywood movies

III. Conclusion: Economic, demographic, and social factors, not television, as the reasons for the decline of Hollywood audiences in post-war America

Sample Sentence Outline

Thesis statement: Although it is common to blame the decline of film audiences on the rise of the medium of television, it was a web of changing economic, demographic, and social factors that caused the decline of Hollywood audiences in post-war America.

I. Introduction: A rising new medium is often blamed for the decline of an older medium
   A. Many blamed radio for the decline in newspaper circulation
   B. Many laid blame on television for the drop in movie theatre attendance in post-war America
   C. Many saw the Internet as the reason for the decline in newspaper circulation

II. Body: Several factors contributed to the decline of Hollywood audiences in post-war America
   A. The post-war economic boom expanded the buying power of American families
      1. GI Bill made low-interest loans available
      2. Young families bought houses in the suburbs away from urban centers
      3. America began its love affair with cars
      4. Mass-produced appliances became affordable

B. Changing demographics contributed to the changing life styles of Americans
1. People married at earlier ages
2. People started families earlier than previous generations

C. Changing economy played a role in changing life-styles
1. Urban areas began to decline
2. A lot of young families started living in the suburbs
3. More families entertained at home
4. Drive-ins allowed for inexpensive suburban family entertainment

D. The quality of Hollywood movies deteriorated

III. Conclusion: Economic, demographic, and social factors all contributed to the decline of Hollywood audiences in post-war America

When using either of the formal outlines, it is important to maintain parallelism in the elements of the same level of subordination. Namely, elements of the same level should have the same grammatical structure (for more information on parallel structures, see Chapter 5, Grammar, Style, and Punctuation Section). Additionally, writers should pay attention to the punctuation conventions of the outlines. While in the sentence outline a period is required after each complete sentence, no punctuation is required after words, phrases, or clauses in the topic outline.

SUPPORTING AN ARGUMENT

As noted earlier, an outline can be a helpful tool not only in organizing the writer's research on a topic, but also in writing up one's findings. The major part of writing a successful media paper lies in the logical presentation of its argument. Typically, a paper addresses one main claim that is expressed in its thesis. When a writer makes a claim, no matter how large or small, it has to be supported by evidence. Information gathered from primary and secondary sources is used as evidence. In addition to the textual information in the form of quotations or paraphrases, writers can also use visual aids, such as tables, graphs, pie charts, and photos, to back up their assertions. Similar to the words, phrases, and ideas borrowed from prior work, visual aids should be properly cited if they are taken from another source. Some visual aids may need special software to make the paper look professional. Before using visual aids in a media paper, writers should consult with their professors or supervisors regarding this option. In some instances, visual aids are incorporated in the text of the paper, in others they are attached as appendices, yet in other cases they may not be appropriate.

As noted before, an argumentative paper presupposes that the writer may not agree with the claims made by some researchers and writers. Disagreement among researchers is part of the process of exploring a topic or issue. However, such a disagreement should be addressed in a polite and respectful manner. The writer should avoid any sarcastic or sneering comments or remarks. Attacking someone's personality instead of pointing out the shortcomings or gaps in that person's research is a strategy writers should shun (see Tannen, 1998). Neither should they misrepresent or simplify someone's findings or claims. Learning how to disagree in a professional manner is part of becoming a media writer.

WRITING EFFECTIVE INTRODUCTIONS AND CONCLUSIONS

The parts of the paper that tend to be revised most are the introduction and conclusion. The two are interconnected—while the introduction presents the main point of the paper, the conclusion underscores its significance. Because they frame the argument of the paper, the importance of the introduction and conclusion should not be overlooked. An effective introduction should orient the reader toward a problem or topic and do so in a clear and engaging manner. To provoke the reader's interest, the writer can start with a striking statistic, an anecdote, or a rhetorical question. To avoid ineffective introductions, the writer should avoid starting a paper with a dictionary definition (e.g., *"Merriam-Webster's Collegiate Dictionary* defines media as . . ."), a sweeping generalization (e.g., "Everybody knows that . . ."), or a research announcement (e.g., "This paper investigates the role of media in . . ."). An effective introduction, in addition to introducing the topic and inciting the reader's interest, should contain a thesis statement. It is not unusual for writers to realize that in the process of writing a paper their topic or argument has shifted slightly, and if that is the case, they should go back and revise the introduction to reflect the change.

The conclusion ties the paper together. It provides an answer to the research question. Some writers, however, "run out of steam" toward the end of the research and writing process, and, as a result, their conclusions are short, choppy, and perfunctory. First, the length of the conclusion should be proportional to the length of the paper. A two-sentence conclusion for a 15-page research paper would not be sufficient, while in two-to-three paragraphs writers are more likely to achieve an effective conclusion of their work. Second, an effective conclusion anticipates and answers the "So what?" question. In other words, it should connect the findings of the paper to the larger idea or problem and, if applicable, provide suggestions for further research. Thus, a writer should be careful not to reduce the conclusion only to a summary of the key points made in the paper. At the same time, the conclusion should not introduce new arguments or evidence that were not covered in the paper. As the products of careful research and thoughtful writing, effective introductions and conclusions are essential ingredients for a successful media paper.

SUMMARY

Writing a strong media paper or professional report depends on having an effective strategy. In this chapter, several key elements for the completion of a successful research paper or professional report have been reviewed.

Of crucial importance is the selection of a topic that can be addressed in the 10- to 15-page paper or report. The one problem most beginning media writers make is to select a topic that is too broad. A narrow research topic allows the media writer to cover the issue with enough detail and evidence within the space available. Exploring a narrow topic in depth reflects a focused research strategy and rigorous thinking. Media writers who attempt to cover a broad topic, on the other hand, tend to present shallow papers that gloss over important points and issues.

The writing process begins with preliminary research. Reviewing sources such as textbooks, encyclopedias, and handbooks is usually the first step in selecting a manageable topic. These sources can help guide the media writer to an appropriate topic and provide a scholarly context for the research project.

Formulating a research question is also important, as it provides a focus point throughout the research and writing phases. Research papers and professional reports are not simply the accumulation of facts, dates, and quotations. Instead, they are a thorough response to a research question. Developing a strong thesis statement, using outlines to present one's research and findings logically and with ample support, constructing an effective introduction and conclusion, all contribute to writing a successful media paper.

In sum, strong media research papers do not happen by chance. They are the result of focused thinking, rigorous research, and disciplined writing. In the following chapter, the reader will find suggestions for improving his or her writing skills.

REFERENCES

Booth, W. C., Colomb, G. G., & Williams, J. M. (2008). *The craft of research* (3rd ed.). Chicago & London: University of Chicago Press.

Brooks, B. S. & The Missouri Group. (1999). *News reporting and writing.* Boston: Bedford/St. Martin's.

Burns, G. (2004). Colorization. In H. Newcomb, *Encyclopedia of television, Museum of Broadcast Communications* (pp. 555–556). New York: Fitzroy Dearborn.

Ford, J. (Director). (1956). *The searchers* [Motion picture]. United States: C. V. Whitney Pictures.

Harrower, T. (2002). *The newspaper designer's handbook* (5th ed.). New York, NY: McGraw-Hill Companies.

Jamieson, K. H. & Campbell, K. K. (2006). *The interplay of influence: News, advertising, politics, and the Internet* (46th ed.). Belmont, CA: Thomson/Wadsworth.

Labov, W. & Fanshel, D. (1977). *Therapeutic discourse: Psychotherapy as conversation.* New York: Academic Press.

Leone, S. (Director). (1966). *The good, the bad and the ugly* [Motion picture]. Italy, Spain, West Germany: Arturo González Producciones Cinematográficas.

Lev, P. (2006). *The fifties: Transforming the screen, 1950–1959* (Vol. 7). History of the American cinema (Series). Berkeley: University of California Press.

Mangold, J. (Director). (2007). *3:10 to Yuma* [Motion picture]. United States: Lionsgate.

McNair, B. (1995). *An introduction to political communication.* New York: Routledge.

Mnookin, S. (2004). *Hard news: Twenty-one brutal months at the* New York Times *and how they changed the American media.* New York: Random House.

Tannen, D. (1998). *The argument culture: Moving from debate to dialogue.* New York: Random House.

Wellman, W. A. (Director). (1943). *The Ox-Bow incident* [Motion picture]. United States: Twentieth Century-Fox Film Corporation.

Zolov, E. (1999). *Refried Elvis: The rise of Mexican counterculture.* Berkeley, CA: University of California Press.

CHAPTER 5

Problems and Solutions

This chapter addresses fundamental writing issues and focuses on some typical problems media writers encounter while researching, writing, editing, and formatting their papers, and offers possible solutions. It begins with a few exploratory exercises aimed at helping writers select a media topic for their papers. Next, the chapter offers a style, grammar, and punctuation guide writers can use as a quick reference when writing, and especially when revising and editing their papers. The guide also reviews examples of specific problems and provides suggestions for solving them. Writers whose first language is not English will find the next section of this chapter, "Tips for ESL Writers," helpful. The chapter continues with an overview of the main formatting styles used for media papers—APA, MLA, and Chicago—followed by a sample page formatted in these three styles. The chapter closes with the checklist writers should use before submitting their final papers.

HELP WITH SELECTING A TOPIC

Some writers find the process of selecting a topic for a paper overwhelming and intimidating. As mentioned earlier (see Chapter 4), writers can review their textbooks and conduct several brainstorming sessions to identify the topic for a media paper. Additionally, writers should not overlook the importance of curiosity and preliminary investigation in the process of selecting a topic. Asking a series of questions and creating hypothetical scenarios about an issue or phenomenon can lead to a topic selection, as well as to the development of a solid research question. Following are four examples of how writers can apply curiosity and imagination to their search for a topic of a media paper.

Example 1

What if print technology had never been developed? Books, newspapers, and magazines, as we know them today, would not exist. Consequently, typical libraries, bookstores, and archives would not exist either. In short, there would be no printed record of the past or the present. Everything would be handwritten. What would such a society be like? How would information be transmitted from one generation to another? This series of questions may lead to the following research question: "How do different societies preserve and transmit cultural knowledge from generation to generation, and what is the role of print media in this process?"

Example 2

Imagine a world without iPods, YouTube, or cell phones. What would life be like in a world without computers, USB flash drives, compact discs (CDs), digital video discs (DVDs), or the Internet? Would it be safer or more dangerous? Would life be easier or harder? Would people be happier? A world without these technological innovations existed only a few decades ago, and we know, from looking at television news footage, and reading newspapers and magazines from that time, that the world of a few decades ago looked a lot different from the world of today. These simple observations demonstrate that media do make a difference in the way people live their lives, relate to others, and come to see themselves. From this observation, writers may develop a specific research question such as, "How was the life of a typical teenager in the early 1900s different from the one in the early 2000s regarding the use of media?" In turn, this question could then lead writers to ask: "How do the media of today affect the lives of teenagers?"

Example 3

This example is also focused on the use of media, but it involves firsthand experience, an experiment of sorts. Try going 24 hours without media. This means no newspapers, radio, magazines, television, iPods, computers, or cell phones. Select a weekend or holiday when living without media will not be detrimental to your work or studies. Like many other professors of mass communication, Raul Tovares, the coauthor of this book, has assigned this exercise to students in his Introduction to Mass Communication class. He explains to them that he does not expect them to live without media for an entire 24-hour period. Rather, the purpose of the exercise is to make students aware of just how pervasive media have become. Trying to live media-free makes people aware of how dependent they are on the media. Most students reported having trouble going one hour without media. Writers can test how long they can go without media. This experiment can lead to several questions that can shape a research project: "How have media changed our lives? Have all of the changes been positive?"

Example 4

As new communication technologies are developed, some researchers are curious about why some are accepted, like television and iPods, and others rejected, like Betamax and 8-Track players. Media researchers are also eager to understand why some technologies are used in ways different from those intended by the persons who first developed them. For example, when cell phones first appeared, it was believed that people would use them primarily to send voice messages. Very quickly, however, text messaging became almost as popular as voice messaging. In addition, cell phone users began using the symbols on the text pad of a cell phone, such as the letters "L" and "O," to send messages (LOL for "laugh out loud") in a code never imagined by the engineers and executives that developed the first cell phones. Writers may ask: "How do people adapt a new technology, such as cell phones, to meet their own everyday needs?"

Earlier still, the initial intention behind Alexander Graham Bell's invention of the telephone was to develop a machine to help the deaf. As a teacher of the deaf, his interest was in helping his students learn. He never imagined putting a telephone in every home. This information begs the following question: "How does a new communication technology deviate from the expectations of its inventor(s) and find acceptance in a broad section of the population?"

Writers can use the provided examples as templates to channel their own curiosity and imagination into the process of selecting a topic that they find interesting. Finding a topic that provokes a writer's interest makes the process of researching and writing more rewarding. Furthermore, when a writer is interested in the topic of his or her paper and enjoys researching and writing about it, there is a better chance that readers will engage with the text as well.

FROM A DRAFT TO A FINISHED PAPER

This section offers a number of strategies for turning a draft into a well-written, polished paper. The goal of this discussion is not to cover every rule; instead, it centers on typical problems and mistakes. As noted in previous chapters, writing a successful media paper means researching a topic, making a valid argument, and supporting it with evidence. However, these important steps will be wasted if a writer fails to communicate his or her findings in an engaging and coherent manner. After all, the goal of writing a paper is to persuade the intended audience that the issue at hand is worth reading about. If the material is poorly organized and presented in a dull or confusing manner, even the strongest argument can be lost.

One mistake novice writers frequently make is confusing their first draft with the finished paper. Once they have everything down on paper, they consider their work done. For experienced writers, on the other hand, their first draft is what it is—a rough copy that needs careful revising and editing. Writing a paper can be compared to moving into a new house. First, it is important to move everything inside the house. Some things find their place right away, while others need to be rearranged to find a better fit, and some items can even be thrown away. In the same fashion, when working on a paper, a writer first has to note down everything that he or she wants to say about the topic. (Having a working outline helps keep the draft focused. See Chapter 4 for more information about outlines). The next step involves revising the draft. The two steps are often intertwined, as many writers revise as they write and write more as they revise. Revisions are done on both the macro (the whole document, its thesis and paragraphs) and micro (individual sentences) levels. Micro-level revisions, or editing, are usually done during the final stages of the document preparation, when writers correct spelling mistakes, grammar, and punctuation errors, and change wording and formatting; macro-level revisions are the starting point of working on a draft. Writers begin by critically examining the relationship between the main point of the paper and its supporting elements; they reorganize and rearrange ideas to ensure a logical flow of the argument, delete irrelevant material, and add new evidence to strengthen their argument. On both macro and micro levels, writers should pay attention to coherence and cohesion.

COHERENCE AND COHESION

Both coherence and cohesion help readers make sense of the text. While cohesion refers to smooth transitions between individual sentences, coherence is understood as linking larger parts of text, such as paragraphs, into a unified whole—a well-organized paper. Williams (2007, p. 80) compares cohesive sentences to neatly fitting pieces of a jigsaw puzzle and a coherent paper to a picture put together out of these pieces. It is the responsibility of the writer to make his or her ideas clear to the reader. Following are a few techniques writers should use to achieve coherence and cohesion:

1. Each paragraph should develop and contribute in a clear and explicit way to the main idea of the paper—: its thesis (see Chapter 4 for more information about thesis development). One way to test paragraph coherence is to underline the topic sentence in each paragraph and then test its relevance to the thesis of the paper.
2. Transitional or linking words connect sentences into a unified paragraph and provide transitions between paragraphs (e.g., *as a result of, for example, nevertheless, similarly, in contrast, in fact, consequently, although, finally, etc.*).

3. Repetition of the key words throughout the text serves as a cohesive device and provides conceptual landmarks for the readers. For instance, if the topic of a paper is *New Media and Their Influence on Teenage Patterns of Communication*, the words *teenagers*, *new media*, and *communication* (and their synonyms) should be used throughout the text.

4. Synonyms help avoid excessive repetition, but allow writers to stay focused on the topic, thus making a paper coherent (e.g., *teenager*, *young person*, *teen*, *adolescent*).

5. Pronouns (e.g., *she*, *he*, *it*, *they*, *we*, *that*, *this*, *those*, *these*) give sentences cohesion without unnecessary repetition (e.g., Many would argue that *Facebook* and *MySpace* transcend social and geographic boundaries. In other words, *they* create a global social community. *These* social-networking sites emerged in 2004 and 2005 and immediately became immensely popular, especially among teenagers.)

Readers appreciate coherent papers because they can easily follow the development of the writer's argument without being distracted or confused. Another important element of a successful paper is its appropriate style.

FORMAL STYLE AND VOCABULARY

On a daily basis, people engage in conversational style shifting. Namely, the same person talks differently with different people and in different settings. In a similar fashion, writers adjust their style depending on the target audience. When one is writing a media paper, the initial intended audience is either a professor or a supervisor. Because the style of such a paper is usually formal, a writer should be careful with the choice of words, writing conventions, and grammar usage. The following are a few tips for ensuring a formal or academic style of writing:

1. Avoid everyday informal words and expressions such as *awesome*, *kids*, *cool*. Instead, use words like *wonderful*, *children*, and *excellent*.

2. Exclude abbreviations such as *u* for *you*, *thru* for *through*, or *r* for *are* that are typical for informal text messaging but are not appropriate for formal writing. The same policy applies to the acronyms BFF, LOL, BTW, and so on.

3. Spell out contractions such as *don't*, *won't*, *it's*: *do not*, *will not*, and *it is*.

4. Exclude all types of profanity.

5. Avoid sexist and other biased language (see following section).

6. Use professional jargon carefully. When introducing a technical term or a concept for the first time, a writer should provide its definition.

POINT OF VIEW

While the previous examples of formal writing are applicable to all papers about media, others, such as point of view, may vary. Point of view, or voice, is linked to how writers refer to themselves and their audience. The choice between using first-, second- or third-person pronouns depends on the established conventions of a particular publication and on the type of information writers are trying to convey. Using the first-person singular pronoun (*I*, *me*, *my*, *mine*), as well as the plural form (*we*, *us*), is usually restricted to those instances when writers discuss personal examples or experiences.

However, some publications allow authors to identify themselves as *I*, instead of the impersonal *the writer* or *the researcher*. Writers can use the second-person pronoun *you* only when giving instructions to the reader. For instance, when the goal of the article is to instruct the audience on how to use a newly released media device or program, the use of *you* can be justified. However, using *you* as a general referring term, such as *when you think about new media technology*, is not suitable for academic or professional writing. The most appropriate pronouns for the formal style of writing are third-person singular (*he*, *she*, *it*) and plural (*they*) pronouns. As noted earlier, the choice of pronominal use depends not only on the content or style of one's paper, but also on the conventions of the publication. Therefore, writers should carefully review a syllabus or publication instructions to choose the most appropriate voice for their papers. Additionally, they may consult with their professors or supervisors. Other strategies of how to achieve a formal writing style include choosing the right verb, using hedges and efficient language, and avoiding biased language.

CHOOSING THE RIGHT VERB

The key element of each sentence is the verb; not only does it make a sentence grammatically correct, but it also conveys information about the action. Therefore, it is not surprising that writers should focus on verb selection to "tighten" their sentences. One way to achieve precision is to substitute phrasal verbs with their single-word synonyms. Phrasal verbs usually consist of a verb followed by a particle to form an idiom, such as *come up*, *look for*, *make up*, *turn down*, *look into*, and others. In the next example, the first sentence has a phrasal verb, while the second contains its synonym.

Original: The reporter *looked into* the allegations of corruption.
Revised: The reporter *investigated* the allegations of corruption.

Not only is the revised sentence more formal in style, it also gives a more precise description of the reporter's actions. Following is a list of common phrasal verbs and their one-word synonyms:

come up—arise
come up with—produce, introduce
make up—reconcile, invent
look forward to—anticipate
turn down—reject, refuse
bring about—cause
put up with—tolerate
do away with—abolish
give up—surrender, renounce, abandon
fight off—resist, repel

For more information about the verb (its form and function), see Kolln and Funk (2009).

USING HEDGES

When working on a paper, writers should carefully balance their certainty with caution (Williams, 2007). Most media topics and ideas cannot be approached with unwavering certainty, but instead require caution and skepticism. Hedges (*potentially*, *likely*, *fairly*, *seem*, *tend*, *suggest*, *may*, *perhaps*, *possibly*, etc.) lessen a writer's certainty by adding a note of caution to the sentences in which confidence may not be fitting. When used sparingly, hedges help writers achieve a more nuanced diction. Compare the following two sentences:

> Original: Nielsen Media Research proves that men watch video on mobile phones, while women watch video on the Internet.
> Revised: Nielsen Media Research *suggests* that men *tend* to watch video on mobile phones, while women are *more likely* to watch video on the Internet.

In contrast to the original sentence, the revised sentence presents the findings of Nielsen Media Research (2008) not as the truth of last resort, but as a nuanced report that is careful enough to avoid sweeping generalizations. Furthermore, the wording of the revised sentence is closer to what the agency actually reported: "Men are more likely than women to watch video on mobile phones, while women are more likely than men to watch video on the Internet" (p. 4). However, writers should not overuse hedges, otherwise they run the risk of making their arguments too wordy and weak.

USING EFFICIENT LANGUAGE

While it is important to express ideas fully and in detail, one's clarity of writing can be compromised by unnecessary wordiness. Therefore, when revising papers, writers should identify and revise excessive verbosity and redundancy. For instance, some long phrases can be expressed in one or two words:

> the reason for—why
> due to the fact that—because
> despite the fact that—even though

with regard to—regarding
at this point in time—now

Redundant phrases, or phrases in which one word implies the other, are also candidates for revision (Williams, 2007). For instance, in the phrase *true facts*, the word *facts* implies that the information is true, thus making the word *true* unnecessary. The following is a list of typical redundant phrases and their more efficient substitutes:

final outcome—outcome
blue in color—blue
consensus of opinion—consensus
completely unanimous—unanimous
oval in shape—oval
future plans—plans
in a careful manner—carefully

When revising, writers should also identify and delete "empty" or meaningless words. In so doing, they not only make their sentences tighter, but they also achieve a more formal style. The following words are considered meaningless and thus can be eliminated without losing the meaning of a sentence: *kind of, actually, rather, basically, practically, particular,* and *virtually.* Yet another way of achieving economy of language is changing negative expressions to the affirmative. Moreover, readers usually perceive affirmative expressions as more formal. Following is a list of negative expressions and their affirmative synonyms:

not the same—different
not easy—difficult
not on time—late
not positive—negative
not to pay attention to—to ignore
not to stop—to continue
not to notice—to overlook

However, if writers intend to emphasize the negative, they do not have to substitute the negative with the affirmative. See

Williams (2007) for more information on how to achieve a clear and concise writing style.

USING UNBIASED LANGUAGE

As mentioned earlier in this chapter, one of the goals of writing a successful media paper is to convince the audience that the topic at hand is worth discussing. However, discussion or engagement with the text is hindered when writers use terms that readers find offensive. In other words, by using biased or exclusionary language, writers can offend and alienate their readers and, as a result, lose credibility and fail to engage in a productive dialogue with readers. Thus writers should carefully review their work to eliminate prejudiced or otherwise offensive language. Next are a few suggestions on how to identify and avoid bias in one's writing.

AVOIDING SEXIST LANGUAGE

Language that unjustly excludes or privileges a particular gender is known as sexist language. Being inclusive in one's writing is not as difficult as some proponents of language "traditions" claim. Moreover, media have been staunch advocates for inclusive language. For instance, in 1984 the Australian Broadcasting Corporation network pioneered the policy of avoiding sexist language. Although some members of both the audience and the media initially opposed this rule, the ABC network adhered to the policy (Leitner, 1997).

Here are a few strategies writers can use to avoid sexist language:

1. Choose a neutral term to refer to professions or occupations. This list offers inclusive alternatives (right) to the job titles that are exclusive (left):
   fireman—firefighter
   policeman—police officer
   chairman—chair, chairperson
   stewardess—flight attendant
   lady doctor—doctor
   male nurse—nurse

2. When gender is not important in describing a person or a group of people, it is advisable to avoid the words that contain *man*:

   mankind—humankind, humanity

   early man—early humans

   every man—every person, every human being

3. Because the English language does not have a gender-neutral third-person singular pronoun that can be used to refer to a person (the third-person pronoun *it* is used for nonhuman referents only), writers have to make conscious efforts to be inclusive in their pronominal usage. Following are a few options writers can use to be inclusive and avoid what is called the *generic he* (*his, him*).

   a. Use the plural.

      Original: A media studies graduate can use his degree to launch a successful career in media advocacy and education.

      Revision: Media studies graduates can use their degrees to launch successful careers in media advocacy and education.

   b. Use *she* or *he* (*his* or *her*; *him* or *her*).

      Original: Every writer should proofread his work.

      Revision: Every writer should proofread his or her work.

   c. Use phrases and clauses that do not require gendered pronouns.

      Original: When a writer investigates media use among teenagers, he should complement interviews with observations.

      Revision 1: When investigating media use among teenagers, the writer should complement interviews with observations.

      Revision 2: A writer who investigates media use among teenagers should complement interviews with observations.

AVOIDING ETHNIC AND RACIAL BIAS

Only when racial or ethnic identification is relevant to the topic of the paper, should writers use such descriptors in reference to a person or a group of people. Furthermore, it is important to choose the term that is preferred by the members of a particular group. For instance, such identifications as *African American, Black, Latino(a), Chicana(o), Hispanic, Mexican American, Native American,* and so forth are some of the appropriate choices.

AVOIDING "LOADED" TERMS

When describing or identifying people, ideas, and organizations, writers should be careful to do so in a neutral manner. They should avoid emotionally charged, value-laden, or "loaded" words and expressions. For instance, a group of people who worship together can be referred to as a *church,* a *religious organization,* or a *cult.* While the first two terms identify this group of people in a neutral way, the last term, a *cult,* immediately frames them negatively. Choosing value-neutral words does not weaken the argument; instead it gives writers an opportunity to engage in a productive and responsible discussion. The following words are examples of value-laden words: *conservative, liberal, cult, gang,* and *primitive.*

SENTENCE LENGTH AND TYPE

While previous sections address revisions on the level of words, this section turns to the revision of sentences. Writers should pay attention to the length and type of sentences they use. For instance, if a paper has an excessive number of either very short or very long sentences, readers may find it choppy or confusing, respectively. Accordingly, while some short sentences can be expanded or merged with other sentences of the same length, very long sentences can be made into two or even three separate sentences. The key in both the length and type of sentences is balance and variety. The type of sentence—simple, compound, and complex—is identified based on the number of clauses and the relationship between them. A clause is a set of one subject and one verb. A simple sentence has one independent clause, or a clause that can form a grammatical sentence: *The reporter left.* It is worth remembering that simple sentences are not synonymous with short sentences; they may be both short (having only essential elements) and long (having optional elements).

Simple short sentence: The NBC Peacock was created in 1956. Simple long sentence: To usher in the era of color television, the NBC Peacock was created in 1956 by John Graham, a native New Yorker and NBC art director.

In contrast to a simple sentence that has only one independent clause, a compound sentence has two or more independent clauses that can be joined together by a semicolon, a comma with a coordinating conjunction (e.g., *and, but, yet*), or a semicolon followed by a conjunctive adverb (e.g., *however, moreover, furthermore*). Compound sentences not only offer sentence variety, but they also help writers demonstrate connections between ideas.

Compound sentence 1: The first official logo of NBC, a microphone surrounded by lightning bolts, first appeared in 1943; the Peacock replaced it in 1956.
Compound sentence 2: The first official logo of NBC, a microphone surrounded by lightning bolts, first appeared in 1943, but the Peacock replaced it in 1956.
Compound sentence 3: The first official logo of NBC, a microphone surrounded by lightning bolts, first appeared in 1943; however, the Peacock replaced it in 1956.

A complex sentence has at least one subordinate, or dependent, clause. Unlike an independent clause, a subordinate clause cannot stand alone—it needs to be attached to an independent clause to form a grammatical sentence—and typically begins with a subordinator such as *while, when, because, although, as,* and *even though*. A complex sentence can either begin or end with a subordinate clause. When a complex sentence begins with a subordinate clause, it should be separated from an independent clause with a comma. However, typically no comma is needed between the two clauses if an independent clause is followed by a dependent clause.

Complex sentence 1: Because most people associate NBC with the peacock, few know that the first official logo of the company was a microphone surrounded by lightning bolts.

Complex sentence 2: Few people know that the first official logo of NBC was a microphone surrounded by lightning bolts because most associate NBC with the peacock.

By using sentences of various types and lengths, writers can communicate their ideas effectively and logically without being monotonous. The following sections address other sentence-level problems that writers should identify and revise.

AVOIDING SENTENCE FRAGMENTS

When a subordinate clause is not preceded or followed by an independent clause, it forms a sentence fragment. While sentence fragments are widespread in everyday speech, in writing they are considered ungrammatical.

Sentence fragment: Because the iPod revolutionized how people buy and listen to music.
Revision 1: Because the iPod revolutionized how people buy and listen to music, fewer people consider investing in home audio systems.
Revision 2: Fewer people consider investing in home audio systems because the iPod revolutionized how people buy and listen to music.
Revision 3: The iPod revolutionized how people buy and listen to music.

PARALLEL STRUCTURES

Another error writers should check for when editing their papers is the absence of parallelism in lists and series. In sentences, parallel structures are connected with the help of commas and/or linking elements known as conjunctions. Specifically, parallel elements in a sentence can be linked by either the coordinating conjunctions (*and, or, but, for*) or correlative conjunctions (*either . . . or, neither . . . nor, not only . . . but also*). It is important that all the elements in a list or series be of the same grammatical form. For instance, if the first element in a series is a noun (a word that refers to a person, thing, or idea), the rest should be nouns too. The following sentences illustrate this point:

Unparallel sentence: To write a good media paper, one needs time, discipline, and to rely on credible sources. (*time* [noun], *discipline* [noun], *to rely* [verb form]—not parallel)

Revised sentence: To write a good media paper, one needs time, discipline, and credible sources. (*time* [noun], *discipline* [noun], *sources* [noun]—parallel)

Parallelism is important not only on a sentence level, but also in the paper outline—sections of the same level should be of the same grammatical structure. For more information about outlines and sample outlines, see Chapter 4.

SENTENCES IN THE PASSIVE VOICE

If a sentence is in the active voice, its subject is the actor who performs the action expressed by the verb. In a passive sentence, the subject is not the doer of the action but instead is its recipient. To achieve a clear description of "who is doing what," writers should use the active voice.

Passive voice: The movie was declared a complete failure by the critics.

Active voice: Critics declared the movie a complete failure.

Many readers would find the active sentence stronger and clearer than its passive version. However, when it is important to place the emphasis on the recipient of the action or when the actor is unknown, using the passive voice is justified. For instance:

Passive voice: The investigative reporter was attacked by the murder suspect.

Passive voice: The video equipment was stolen.

In sum, passive sentences are not ungrammatical, but because they are typically more vague and wordy than active sentences, they should be used sparingly.

SUBJECT-VERB AGREEMENT

Subject-verb agreement errors are among the most common grammar mistakes. Subject-verb agreement is achieved when the subject and the verb of a sentence agree in number and person.

A *reporter contacts* police officers, city officials, and community leaders for potential story leads. (Both the subject, *reporter*, and the verb, *contacts*, are singular.)

Reporters contact police officers, city officials, and community leaders for potential story leads. (Both the subject and the verb are plural.)

While writers can easily notice subject-verb agreement errors in sentences where the verb immediately follows the simple subject, they should pay close attention to sentences with compound subjects (when the subject consists of two or more elements), post-noun modifiers (when the subject is followed by a word or words that describe it), and nonessential elements separating the subject from the verb. For instance, if the subject is compound and its elements are connected by conjunctions (*and, both . . . and, not only . . . but also*), the verb should be plural in number.

Original: Television and the Internet *is* mass media.
Revised: Television and the Internet *are* mass media.

However, if the elements of the compound subject are joined together by the conjunctions *or, either . . . or, neither . . . nor*, the verb agrees with the closest noun—the proximity rule.

Original: Neither the director nor the producers *has* complete control over the film.
Revised: Neither the director nor the producers *have* complete control over the film.

However, the proximity rule does not apply when the noun that is closest to the verb is not the subject but an element of a post-noun modifier. For example, in the following sentences, the noun *collection*, not *posters*, is the subject, and the phrase *of 1930s movie posters* modifies that subject.

> Original: The collection of 1930s movie posters *are* on display at the museum.
> Revised: The collection of the 1930s movie posters *is* on display at the museum.

When inserted between the subject and the verb, a nonessential structure does not influence the subject-verb agreement. Such nonessential structures may begin with *as well as, along with, including, together with, in addition to,* and so forth, and are typically enclosed in commas.

> Original: The Internet, along with television and radio, *provide* access to the local news.
> Revised: The Internet, along with television and radio, *provides* access to the local news.

The indefinite subjects, such as *somebody, everybody, nobody, no one, everyone, one,* are treated as singular.

> Original: Nobody in the focus group *like* the new ad campaign.
> Revised: Nobody in the focus group *likes* the new ad campaign.

Collective nouns, such as *family, audience, team, jury,* and *committee,* are treated as singular when they refer to a group of people as a single unit, but they can take the plural form when emphasizing individuals in the group.

> The jury was impressed with the quality of this independent film. (*jury as a unit*)
> The jury were discussing the results of their voting in the "Best Comedy" category. (*individual members of the jury*)

PRONOUN-ANTECEDENT AGREEMENT

Another typical grammar mistake involves pronoun-antecedent agreement. Similarly to how the subject and the verb have to agree in number and person, the pronoun has to agree in both number and person with the noun that it substitutes (the antecedent). For instance, in the original sentence the antecedent, the noun *writer* (third person), does not agree in person with the pronoun *you* (second person).

Original: When *a writer* works on a paper about mass media, *you* should be familiar with relevant literature.

Revised 1: When *a writer* works on a paper about mass media, *he or she* should be familiar with relevant literature. (*a writer*—third person, singular; *he or she*—third person, singular)

Revised 2: When *writers* work on papers about mass media, *they* should be familiar with relevant literature. (*writers*—third person, plural; *they*—third person, plural)

The next example shows an error in which the pronoun does not agree with the noun in number:

Original: Every *citizen* would like to have *their* opinion represented in the media.

Revised: Every *citizen* would like to have *his or her* opinion represented in the media.

Citizen is singular, so *his or her* (singular) should be used.

Finally, the meaning of a sentence is ambiguous when a pronoun has no clear antecedent. In the following example, it is not clear whether *it* refers to the movie itself or critics' evaluation of this movie.

Original: The critics found the movie disappointing, and the fans did not like it.

Revised: The critics found the movie disappointing, and the fans did not like the critics' evaluation.

PUNCTUATION

Careful punctuation alerts readers to the different parts of a sentence, as well as their significance and relationship. In this way, punctuation adds to the effectiveness of individual sentences and contributes to the overall quality of one's paper. Reading out loud and paying attention to the pauses and changes in tempo can help writers punctuate their papers; however, it is knowledge of punctuation conventions that gives them confidence in doing so. While punctuation conventions are perhaps less stringent than those of grammar and spelling, there are a few basic rules that every writer should know and follow. The following is a brief overview of some punctuation conventions; for a more comprehensive review of punctuation, writers should consult one of the suggested grammar handbooks (see Chapter 6).

Do not Separate the Subject and the Verb with a Single Comma

Writers usually make this mistake when the subject has either compound elements or extensive modifiers.

Original: Both the network and cable television programs in the 1980s and 1990s, became more sensationalistic and ratings-driven.

Revised: Both the network and cable television programs in the 1980s and 1990s became more sensationalistic and ratings-driven.

Avoid Comma Splices and Run-On Sentences

Two independent clauses (see p. 141) cannot be combined into a compound sentence with a single comma alone (a comma splice) or without any punctuation at all (a run-on sentence).

Comma splice: Each year, companies in the United States spend $200 billion on advertising, its impact on the target audience remains controversial.

Run-on sentence: Each year, companies in the United States spend $200 billion on advertising its impact on the target audience remains controversial.

Revision 1: Each year, companies in the United States spend $200 billion on advertising, but its impact on the target audience remains controversial. (*comma + conjunction*)

Revision 2: Each year, companies in the United States spend $200 billion on advertising; its impact on the target audience remains controversial. (*semicolon*)

Revision 3: Each year, companies in the United States spend $200 billion on advertising; however, its impact on the target audience remains controversial. (*semicolon + conjunctive adverb + comma*)

Signal Nonessential Elements by Enclosing Them in Commas, Dashes, or Parentheses

The elements of a sentence that provide information that is not crucial to identify a particular person, object, or action are understood as nonessential elements. Such elements provide additional commentary or rename a word or words that come before them and are typically set off by a comma (at the beginning or end of a sentence) or commas (in the middle of a sentence), as in Example 1. Instead of commas, writers can use dashes to place a bit more emphasis on such elements, as in Example 2. To downplay such elements, parentheses can be used, as shown in Example 3.

Example 1: The cofounders of Google, *Sergey Brin and Larry Page*, met when they were students at Stanford University.

Example 2: Mass media—*television, film, radio, press, and the Internet*—offer limitless topics for research.

Example 3: Three of the major television networks (*ABC, CBS, and NBC*) participated in the Stand up to Cancer initiative.

Signal Sentence Openers with a Comma

A sentence opener is set off by a comma if it is a commentary on the entire sentence and not on a particular element of the sentence (Example 1), an introductory verb phrase (Example 2), a long prepositional phrase that is a phrase that begins with a preposition such as *in, from, to, on, above, at, of, after, before*, and others (Example 3), or a subordinate clause (Example 4).

Example 1: *Apparently*, many young people cannot imagine their lives without cell phones.

Example 2: *To test the viewers' response to food commercials*, the researchers set up an experiment.
Example 3: *After a long and successful acting career*, Clint Eastwood has proven himself to be a talented director.
Example 4: *Because many believe that children emulate behaviors they witness around them*, violence in film and television remains a controversial issue.

Separate Elements in a Series With a Comma

In academic writing, a comma is used to separate elements in a series, including the last element preceded by a coordinating conjunction.

Example: Many film directors also write, produce, and star in their movies.

Use Hyphens and Dashes Appropriately

While hyphens connect separate words into a compound word, dashes signal relationships between larger chunks of text: phrases and clauses. A hyphen is a short punctuation mark (-), while a dash is a longer symbol (—).

Example (hyphen): A number of studies have investigated the role of media in Spanish-speaking communities in the United States.
Example (dash): Although often overlooked as mere vandalism, graffiti is a means of communication—a powerful example of alternative media.

Use a Comma to Signal Direct Quotations

When writers introduce direct quotations after or before verbs such as *tell, suggest, write,* or *report,* they should separate the verb from the quoted material with a comma. The next examples follow the in-text APA citation style:

Example 1: Fraley (2009) suggests, "Hip hop renders visible the complexities of racial identities" (p. 39).
Example 2: "Hip hop renders visible the complexities of racial identities," writes Fraley (2009, p. 39).

However, when quoted material is seamlessly integrated into the structure of a sentence, it does not need an introductory comma.

Example: Fraley (2009) views hip hop as a site of social construction of race because it "renders visible the complexities of racial identities" (p. 39).

Use an Apostrophe to Signal Possession and Contraction

To signal possession in the nouns that form plural with the help of the inflection -s (e.g., a journalist—journalists), the apostrophe is added before the inflection -s when the noun is in singular form and after the inflection -s when the noun is in plural form.

Example 1 (singular): The *journalist's* life was in danger.
Example 2 (plural): The *journalists'* lives were in danger.

In the nouns that form plural without adding the inflection -s—that is, irregularly—writers should signal possession by adding the apostrophe followed by the inflection -s to both the singular and plural forms of the noun.

Example 1: The influence of television on a *child's* development is still being researched.
Example 2: The influence of television on *children's* development is still being researched.

When there are two or more nouns, joint ownership is demonstrated by making possessive only the last noun, while an individual ownership is signaled by making possessive each of the nouns.

Example 1 (their joint work): The news director reviewed *the reporter and photographer's* work.
Example 2 (their work as individuals): The news director reviewed *the reporter's and photographer's* work.

The apostrophe is also used to signal a contraction; when two words are joined together, the omitted letters are replaced by an apostrophe.

> Example (do not—don't): Some people *don't* realize the danger of texting while driving.
> The omission of letters in common phrases can be represented by an apostrophe: *rock 'n' roll.* Another example: The basketball team was *smokin'.*
> *Writing Tip: Pronouns that show possession—ours, yours, his, hers, its, theirs—do not have the apostrophe.*

FINAL EDIT: CHECKING FOR MISTAKES SPELL CHECK CANNOT DETECT

The first type of such mistakes involves homonyms, or words that sound alike but have different spellings and meanings. Some of these homonyms involve contracted forms (see previous example). When revising, writers should pay special attention to such words. Following is a list of the most frequently confused homonyms:

> its—it's
> than—then
> there—their—they're
> too—to—two
> your—you're
> who's—whose

Even experienced writers sometimes confuse the words in the following pairs, but as Williams (2007) observes, understanding distinctions between them can "testify to your precision" (p. 26).

> affect—effect
> among—between
> annoy—aggravate
> anticipate—expect
> compliment—complement

constitute—comprise
continuous—continual
disinterested—uninterested
finalize—finish
notorious—famous

The meanings and usage of these words are described in dictionaries. Writers should always have a copy of a dictionary handy and consult it whenever they are in doubt regarding the meaning or usage of a word. For instance, after consulting *Merriam-Webster's Collegiate Dictionary*, writers will know that in the last pair, the word *notorious* means "widely and unfavorably known" (p. 848), while the word *famous* denotes "widely known; honored for achievement" (p. 452) and will not confuse the two.

TIPS FOR ESL WRITERS

While writing is one of the universal ways of exchanging ideas, different languages and sociocultural practices have contributed to a variety of writing conventions in different countries. This section offers a few tips on how to write papers "American style" for writers whose first language is not English. Some writers who are native speakers of English, but who are not familiar with American academic and professional styles of writing, may find this section helpful as well.

Tip 1.

The main feature of American formal writing is that it is reader-oriented, not writer-oriented (see Langosch, 1996). This means that it is the writer's responsibility to facilitate readers' engagement with the text by producing a clear and coherent paper. (See previous section on grammar and style for more information.)

Tip 2.

Most papers in North America, especially academic texts, are deductive. As Scollon & Scollon (1995) note, a deductive rhetorical structure entails a clear thesis statement at the onset of one's paper. The authors further suggest that the place of the thesis is in correlation with the length of the document; while writers may delay a thesis statement in a book, in a short essay the thesis is expected in the first or second paragraph.

Tip 3.

When working on a paper, a writer should carefully balance his or her ideas and those of others. Because it is extremely rare for a writer to find a topic that has never been studied before, a paper—a research paper in particular—should include an overview of prior work on the subject matter and a writer's contribution to the discussion. In other words, a paper should be neither a mere compilation of others' work nor a writer's solo contribution that disregards prior texts, but rather an engaging dialog between a writer and preceding authors.

Tip 4.

ESL writers should be especially careful to separate their words from those of others by using proper citation conventions. In other words, writers should give credit to people whose words or ideas they use. North American copyright law is very strict, and plagiarism is a serious offence. For instance, students who are caught plagiarizing can be either suspended or even expelled from a college or university (see Plagiarism section in Chapter 3).

Tip 5.

Although it might be difficult in the beginning, ESL writers should write their notes and drafts in English and not in their native languages (Langosch, 1996). Writing first in a different language and then translating the document into English is disadvantageous for several reasons. First, it takes more time and effort to write in one language and then to translate one's work into English than to write in English from the start. Second, by writing in native languages, writers slow down the development of their English grammar, style, and professional vocabulary. Finally, when translating a paper into English, writers are more likely to preserve expressions and sentence structures that are typical for their native languages, but would be unusual or ungrammatical in English. Such mistakes are known as language transfer errors.

Tip 6.

One of the common language transfer errors involves word order in a sentence. This issue especially concerns ESL writers whose native languages have different word order patterns than those of English. English word order in declarative sentences is rather fixed: Subject—Verb—Object (SVO). For instance: *The journalists (S) discussed (V) the proposal (O)*. Adjectives (Adj) precede nouns (N): *a new (Adj) gadget (N)*. Additionally, information about place typically comes before that of time: *The journalists discussed the proposal at the conference (place) on Friday (time)*. (See Maimon, Peritz, & Yancey, 2005) for more information on English grammar and sentence structure.)

Tip 7.

If writers experience problems or have questions about their papers, they should contact their professors or supervisors. For instance, in American colleges and universities, students are encouraged to see their professors during the designated office hours to discuss any issues or problems related to papers or other assignments. It would be a mistake to wait for a professor or a supervisor to initiate such a meeting.

Tip 8.

ESL writers can benefit from having a native speaker review their drafts. To do so, writers can go to a writing center on campus or set up a "language partner" relationship: An ESL writer can tutor an English speaker in a foreign language, while a native speaker can help the ESL writer identify problems in a paper.

Tip 9.

Although this book has essential information on English grammar and style, ESL writers should also invest in a comprehensive grammar and style handbook (see bibliography/suggested readings, Chapter 6).

FORMATTING STYLES

Style refers to how the research paper will look when it is finished. Rules for formatting papers are designed to help writers convey their information as clearly as possible. These styles follow long traditions that make it easier to communicate with readers and help them focus on the content of a paper and follow its flow of ideas (*Publication Manual of the American Psychological Association*, 2001, p. 4). Formats are taken very seriously in academic and professional spheres. Most professors and supervisors will provide detailed information about what they expect in terms of the style, or format, of the research paper. The class syllabus, or perhaps a separate handout about the paper, will include information about the required documentation style. For instance, media professors usually want their students to adhere to one of the following styles: American Psychological Association (APA), Modern Language Association (MLA), or Chicago. There are other styles, but these three are the most frequently used in the field of media studies. The different documentation styles follow different rules of how a document should look, also known as the format, so it is important to know the rules of the required style and be consistent in its use. Formatting rules dictate such things as what information appears on the cover page and how it appears, how sources are cited in the body of text, and how references are listed. The preferred style often reflects a long-standing tradition in a particular area of study; therefore, the formatting style of a paper depends on the class and the professor teaching the class. The APA style is likely to be the preferred choice for a class on the role of media in society. A class on the history of the mass media will likely require the Chicago citation style. A media studies course on the aesthetics of French New Wave films may require following the MLA style. Writers should become familiar with the conventions of the style required for the paper early in the writing process because this will save them time, especially during the last weeks and days of working on a project when they are preparing the final draft for submission.

There are various computer programs that will put an in-text reference and bibliography into the appropriate format. EndNote is one such program that is usually available at university bookstores. Another type of software that is designed to help writers organize and format sources is Noodle Tools (http://www.noodletools.com/). Many university and city libraries subscribe to one or more of such software programs. Writers should ask a librarian or attend a library orientation to take advantage of all the style/formatting resources that a library offers. In addition to formatting software, some word-processing programs, such as Microsoft Word 2007, have reference tools that can help writers insert endnotes, footnotes, and citations into the document, as well as format their bibliography. While formatting programs and tools are helpful, they may not be available or may malfunction when writers need them most. Therefore, a good writer should always have a backup plan and know where she or he can obtain reliable information about formatting styles. Each of these styles—APA, MLA, and Chicago—have hard copies of their manuals of style with exhaustive information about a respective documentation model (the *Publication Manual of the American Psychological Association*, the *MLA Handbook for Writers of Research Papers*, *The Chicago Manual of Style*). Most libraries have one or two copies of the latest editions of such manuals on their reference shelves. Additionally, almost every writing reference book includes a section or a chapter (usually near the end of the book) with information on how to cite and arrange a bibliography using a particular style or styles; some may even include a sample paper or pages, as does this book (see pp. 158–162).

Writers can also find help online. Both the American Psychological Association and Modern Language Association provide links to their respective citation conventions on their Web sites. Thus, if writers need help with the APA style, they can find answers to many of their questions by accessing the following link: http://www.apastyle.org/apa-style-help.aspx. In a similar way, the following link provides assistance with the MLA style: http://www.mla.org/style. Many university writing centers' Web sites offer helpful tips and information for writers, including different formatting guides. For instance, the Writing Center at the University of Wisconsin-Madison offers the following comprehensive review of Chicago/

Turabian documentation style: http://writing.wisc.edu/Handbook/ DocChicago.htmlhttp://writing.wisc.edu/Handbook/DocChicago.html.

Additionally, many online reference sources provide citation suggestions. For example, the *Encyclopædia Britannica* offers citations in both the APA and MLA styles for all of its entries. Thus, its entry "television" is followed by the following citations:

> APA Style: television. (2009). In Encyclopædia Britannica. Retrieved April 26, 2009, from Encyclopædia Britannica Online: http://www.britannica.com/EBchecked/topic/586142/television
> MLA Style: "television." Encyclopædia Britannica. 2009. Encyclopædia Britannica Online. 26 Apr. 2009 <http://www.britannica .com/EBchecked/topic/586142/television>.

In sum, writers have an abundance of sources they can use to format their papers in the required style. If writers are given the option of selecting a documenting style themselves, they should choose the style with which they are most comfortable and familiar. However, once writers select a particular style, they should be consistent and follow the selected style throughout the paper.

Following are three examples of a sample page formatted in accordance with the requirements of three documentation styles: APA, MLA, and Chicago.

Sample Page, APA Format

Post-war movies and television 3

Did television "kill" the movie theater in post-war America?

In the post-war years, one manifestation of a changing American culture was the unprecedented growth of consumer spending on household appliances, including TV sets. While in 1946 only 0.02 percent of American households owned a TV set, by 1955 more than 64 percent were proud owners of this growing media technology (Edgerton, 2007, p. 103). At the same time, movie theaters were witnessing a steady decline in attendance. Between 1946 and

1956, movie theatre audiences decreased by almost 50 percent (Lev, 2006, p. 7). At first glance, these two phenomena appear to be directly linked: Many people stopped going to movie theaters because they enjoyed watching television at home.

A closer examination of the era of television expansion reveals that television was not the principal reason behind the decline of ticket sales for movie theaters. As Manchel (1990) argues, the public and some scholars are quick to identify the new medium of television as the main reason for the decline in movie theater attendance, but they fail to include other important factors such as "removal of wartime shortages, the population shift to the suburbs, the rise of drive-ins, increasing traffic congestion in downtown areas, and the alleged deterioration of film content in the late 1940s" (pp. 648–649). Campbell, Martin, and Fabos (2010, pp. 235–236), following Gomery (1991), suggest that the decline in movie attendance began several years before the popularization of television as a form of popular entertainment in the late 1940s. Although it is common to blame the decline of one medium on the rise of a new one, it was not television but a web of economic, demographic, and social factors that caused the decline of Hollywood audiences in post-war America.

References

Campbell, R., Martin, C. R., & Fabos, B. (2010). *Media and culture: An introduction to mass communication*. Boston and New York: Bedford/ St. Martin's.

Edgerton, G. R. (2007). *The Columbia history of American television*. New York: Columbia University Press.

Gomery, D. (1991). Who killed Hollywood? *Wilson Quarterly, 15* (3), 106–112. Retrieved June 12, 2009, from Academic Search Premier database.

Lev, P. (2006). *The fifties: Transforming the screen, 1950–1959* (Vol. 7). History of the American cinema (Series). Berkeley: University of California Press.

Manchel, F. (1990). *Film study: An analytical bibliography* (Vol. 1). Cranbury, NJ: Fairleigh Dickinson University Press.

Sample Page, MLA Format

Smith 1

Did Television "Kill" the Movie Theater in Post-War America?

In the post-war years, one manifestation of a changing American culture was the unprecedented growth of consumer spending on household appliances, including TV sets. While in 1946 only 0.02 percent of American households owned a TV set, by 1955 more than 64 percent were proud owners of this growing media technology (Edgerton 103). At the same time, movie theaters were witnessing a steady decline in attendance. Between 1946 and 1956, movie theatre audience decreased by almost 50 percent (Lev 7). At first glance, these two phenomena appear to be directly linked: many people stopped going to movie theaters because they enjoyed watching television at home.

A closer examination of the era of television expansion reveals that television was not the principal reason behind the decline of ticket sales for movie theaters. As Manchel argues, the public and some scholars are quick to identify the new medium of television as the main reason for the decline in movie theatre attendance, but they fail to include other important factors such as "removal of wartime shortages, the population shift to the suburbs, the rise of drive-ins, increasing traffic congestion in downtown areas, and the alleged deterioration of film content in the late 1940s" (648–649). Campbell, Martin, and Fabos (235–236), following Gomery, suggest that the decline in movie attendance began several years before the popularization of television as a form of popular entertainment in the late 1940s. Although it is common to blame the decline of one medium on the rise of a new one, it was not television but a web of economic, demographic, and social factors that caused the decline of Hollywood audiences in post-war America.

Works Cited

Campbell, Richard, Christopher R. Martin, and Bettina Fabos. *Media and Culture: An Introduction to Mass Communication*. Boston and New York: Bedford/St. Martin's, 2010.

Edgerton, Gary R. *The Columbia History of American Television*. New York: Columbia University Press, 2007.

Gomery, Douglas. Who killed Hollywood? *Wilson Quarterly* 15.3 (1991): 106–112. Retrieved June 12, 2009, from Academic Search Premier database.

Lev, Peter. *The Fifties: Transforming the Screen, 1950–1959*. History of the American Cinema Series. Vol. 7. Berkeley: University of California Press, 2006.

Manchel, Frank. *Film Study: An Analytical Bibliography*. Vol. 1. Cranbury, NJ: Fairleigh Dickinson University Press, 1990.

Sample Page, Chicago Format

Smith 2

Did Television "Kill" the Movie Theater in Post-War America?

In the post-war years, one manifestation of a changing American culture was the unprecedented growth of consumer spending on household appliances, including TV sets. While in 1946 only 0.02 percent of American households owned a TV set, by 1955 more than 64 percent were proud owners of this growing media technology.[1] At the same time, movie theatres were witnessing a steady decline in attendance. Between 1946, and 1956, movie theater audience decreased by almost 50 percent.[2] At first glance, these two phenomena appear to be directly linked: many people stopped going to movie theaters because they enjoyed watching television at home.

A closer examination of the era of television expansion reveals that television was not the principal reason behind the decline of ticket sales for movie theaters. As Manchel argues, the public and some scholars are quick to identify the new medium of television as the main reason for the decline in movie theater attendance, but they fail to include other important factors such as "removal of wartime shortages, the population shift to the suburbs, the rise of drive-ins, increasing traffic congestion in downtown areas, and the alleged deterioration of film content in the late 1940s."[3] Campbell, Martin, and Fabos,[4] following Gomery,[5] suggest that the decline in movie attendance began several years before the popularization of television as a form of popular entertainment in the late 1940s. Although it is common to blame the decline of one medium on the rise of a new one, it was not television but a web of economic, demographic, and social factors that caused the decline of Hollywood audiences in post-war America.

Notes

1. Gary Edgerton, *The Columbia History of American Television* (New York: Columbia University Press, 2007), 103.

2. Peter Lev, *The Columbia History of American Television*, History of the American Cinema Series, vol. 7 (New York: Columbia University Press, 2007), 7.

3. Frank Manchel, *Film Study: An Analytical Bibliography*, vol. 1 (Cranbury, NJ: Fairleigh Dickinson University Press, 1990), 648–649.

4. Richard Campbell, Christopher R. Martin, and Bettina Fabos. *Media and Culture: An Introduction to Mass Communication* (Boston and New York: Bedford/St. Martin's, 2010), 235–236.

5. Douglas Gomery, "Who Killed Hollywood?" *Wilson Quarterly* 15, no. 3 (1991) http://web.ebscohost.com.cassell.founders.howard.edu/ehost/detail? vid=7&hid=5&sid=42880357-116e-4fd4-aeab-8774e106e67d%40sessionmgr 12&bdata=JmxvZ2lucGFnZT1Mb2dpbi5hc3Amc2l0ZT1laG9zdC1saXZl#db =aph&AN=9608281892 (accessed June 12, 2009.)

Bibliography

Campbell, Richard, Christopher R. Martin, and Bettina Fabos. *Media and Culture: An Introduction to Mass Communication.* Boston and New York: Bedford/St. Martin's, 2010.

Edgerton, Gary R. *The Columbia History of American Television.* New York: Columbia University Press, 2007.

Gomery, Douglas. "Who Killed Hollywood?" *Wilson Quarterly* 15, no. 3 (1991): 106–112. http://web.ebscohost.com.cassell.founders.howard. edu/ehost/detail?vid=7&hid=5&sid=42880357-116e-4fd4-aeab-8774e 106e67d%40sessionmgr12&bdata=JmxvZ2lucGFnZT1Mb2dpbi5hc3 Amc2l0ZT1laG9zdC1saXZl#db=aph&AN=9608281892 (accessed June 12, 2009.).

Lev, Peter. *The Fifties: Transforming the Screen, 1950–1959.* History of the American Cinema Series, vol. 7. Berkeley: University of California Press, 2006.

Manchel, Frank. *Film Study: An Analytical Bibliography.* Vol. 1. Cranbury, NJ: Fairleigh Dickinson University Press, 1990.

USING CHECKLIST FOR FINAL PAPERS

The following checklist is a tool writers should use before submitting their final papers. Even though some items on the checklist may seem tedious, writers should treat them with the same degree of importance. Because with time writers become so familiar with the look and content of their papers, they may easily overlook the most obvious mistakes, errors, and omissions. To make the most out of this checklist, writers should photocopy and review a copy of the checklist at the very beginning of the writing-and-research project and periodically check their progress against the checklist. A few days before the paper is due, a writer should critically and methodically address each point included on the checklist.

CHECKLIST FOR MEDIA RESEARCH PAPERS

Formatting

___ My paper meets the required number of pages or words.

___ My paper follows the required spacing (usually double spaced).

___ My paper follows the required size and type of font (typically 12-point Times New Roman).

___ The pages are numbered (some styles also require a running head with either the name of the author [MLA, Chicago] or the title or the partial title of the paper [APA]).

___ The document includes my name and, if applicable, my instructor's name, course number/section, and the date.

Revision

___ My paper contains the title that reflects the main argument of the paper.

___ My paper includes Introduction, Body, and Conclusion.

___ My Introduction triggers my reader's interest in the Body of my paper.

___ My Conclusion ties the paper together and provides an answer to the research question.

___ My paper has a clearly stated thesis.

___ Each paragraph has one main point (a topic sentence) that relates to the thesis of the paper.

___ I define the concepts and terms I use in my paper.

___ I provide enough evidence to support my thesis.

___ I give credit to prior works and authors: I do not plagiarize.

___ I carefully consider opposing points of view: I do not misrepresent or simplify.

___ I take into consideration the opinions, attitudes, and values of my audience.

Editing

___ I use transitions to connect paragraphs and sentences.

___ My sentences are diverse in structure.

___ My choice of words and expressions reflects the formal style of writing.

___ My quotations and references follow the required style (APA, MLA, Chicago, etc.).

___ The references I include in my bibliography can be found in the body of text and vice versa.

___ I have proofread to correct spelling mistakes.

___ I have proofread to correct grammar mistakes (subject-verb agreement, pronoun-antecedent agreement, sentence fragments, run-on sentences, misplaced modifiers, punctuation errors, etc.).

Protecting My Work

___ I have saved a copy of my paper on the hard drive of my computer and on a flash drive, and I have sent a copy to myself as an email attachment.

SUMMARY

A strong media paper or report does not happen overnight, nor does it happen automatically. Every step, from selecting a topic to selecting a verb, involves making deliberate and careful choices. This chapter, in anticipation of some of the problems and issues writers may encounter, offers sample strategies of how to use one's curiosity to find a manageable and interesting topic and practical information for turning one's draft into a well-written paper.

Writers should always be mindful of their audience and write in an appropriate style. An appropriate style for a media paper, in most instances is a formal or academic style, requires writers to pay attention to their choices of words, expressions, points of view, and grammar. Careful punctuation also contributes to the overall quality of one's paper. Furthermore, by writing with precision and grace, writers communicate their ideas clearly and in this way earn respect from their readers.

Every writer encounters problems in the process of researching and writing a paper. By identifying and addressing problems, media writers will not only produce successful papers and reports, but they will also become more confident writers and researchers. In this chapter, sample problems and solutions are aimed at providing writers with the essentials of style, grammar, and punctuation. ESL writers may come across different problems than those experienced by native speakers. In this regard, this chapter offers a set of tips specifically designed for writers whose first language is other than English. In sum, to write a polished paper, a writer should dedicate enough time and effort to each stage of the research-and-writing process—from finding a topic to editing the final draft.

REFERENCES

Campbell, R., Martin, C. R., & Fabos, B. (2010). *Media and culture: An introduction to mass communication*. Boston and New York: Bedford/ St. Martin's.

Edgerton, G. R. (2007). *The Columbia history of American television*. New York: Columbia University Press.

Fraley, T. (2009). I got a natural skill . . .: Hip-hop, authenticity, and whiteness. *The Howard Journal of Communications*, 20: 37–54.

Gomery, D. (1991). Who killed Hollywood? *Wilson Quarterly*, *15* (3), 106–112. Retrieved June 12, 2009, from Academic Search Premier database.

Kolln, M. & Funk, R. (2009). *Understanding English grammar* (8th ed.). New York: Pearson Education.

Langosch, S. L. (1996). *Writing a research paper American style: An ESL handbook*. Hauppauge, NY: Barron's.

Leitner, G. (1997). The sociolinguistics of communication media. In F. Coulmas (Ed.), *The handbook of sociolinguistics* (pp. 187–204). Cambridge, MA.: Blackwell.

Lev, P. (2006). *The fifties: Transforming the screen, 1950–1959.* (Vol. 7). History of the American cinema (Series). Berkeley: University of California Press.

Maimon, E. P., Peritz, J. H., & Yancey, K. B. (2005). *The new McGraw-Hill handbook.* Boston: McGraw Hill.

Manchel, F. (1990). *Film study: An analytical bibliography* (Vol. 1). Cranbury, NJ: Fairleigh Dickinson University Press.

Merriam-Webster's collegiate dictionary (11th ed.). (1993). Springfield, MA: Merriam-Webster.

Neilsen Media Research (2008). A2/M2 three screen report. http://blog.nielsen.com/nielsenwire/wp-content/uploads/2008/11/nielsen_three_screen_report_3q08.pdf

Publication manual of the American psychological association. (5th ed.) (2001). Washington, DC: American Psychological Association.

Scollon, R. & Scollon, S. W. (1995). *Intercultural communication.* Malden, MA & Oxford, UK: Blackwell Publishers.

Williams, J. (2007). *Style: Lessons in clarity and grace* (9th ed.). New York & Boston: Pearson/Longman.

CHAPTER 6

Resources for the Future

This chapter offers an annotated bibliography of resources useful for media writers. It is not intended to be comprehensive, but rather to give the reader an idea of the variety of sources available to those writing about the media. The chapter consists of two main sections: *Print Resources* and *Electronic Resources*. The print section is further divided into several subsections that list references to media books and handbooks, encyclopedias, as well as writing and research resources. *Media Texts*, the first subsection, lists the works that are often cited by media scholars and considered important in the study of media. It also includes several handbooks writers can use to get a general introduction to media studies. The next subsection provides information about encyclopedias that deal with various aspects of media. In the *Research and Writing Texts* subsection, media writers can find information about how to carry out a research project and how to turn one's research into a successful media paper. This section also includes style and grammar resources. The *Electronic Resources* section provides writers with a list of Web addresses along with brief annotations of helpful online tools for media writers. It begins with a list of online writing resources followed by two subsections that focus on research. The first offers an overview of several electronic research databases, while the second focuses specifically on media and media-related research. As with all online sources, the resources listed in the *Electronic Resources* section may or may not be accessible after publication of this book.

PRINT RESOURCES

Media Texts

Writers who want or need information about the key media concepts, issues, and theories will find the following resources useful.

Anderson, B. (1991). *Imagined communities: Reflections on the origin and spread of nationalism*. London: Verso.

Anderson outlines the relationship of print capitalism to the rise of national identity. The media he analyzes are language and newspapers and their contribution to nation building. This book popularized the term *imagined communities*. An essential reference for those who write about national identity as well as ethnic identity and media.

Czitrom, D. J. (1982). *Media and the American mind: From Morse to McLuhan*. Chapel Hill: University of North Carolina.

Using the writings of U.S. and Canadian scholars from the 1800s through the 1960s, Czitrom traces the development of electronic media, from the telegraph through television. A good source for understanding media in a cultural context.

Downing, J., McQuail, D., Schlesinger, P., & Wartella, E. (Eds.). (2004). *The SAGE handbook of media studies*. Thousand Oaks, CA: Sage.

An excellent source for an overview of the state of media studies. The handbook covers a variety of media subjects. Included are topics such as media ethics, advertising, popular music, digital technologies, Bollywood and Indian cinema, and alternative media. A list of references follows every chapter. Author and Subject indexes are also helpful for tracking down researchers and subjects across the different chapters. One volume, 26 chapters cover a broad spectrum of media topics.

Eisenstein, E. L. (1979). *The printing press as an agent of change: Communications and cultural transformations in early modern Europe* (Vols. 1–2). Cambridge, UK: Cambridge University Press.

One of the most thorough accounts of the impact of the printing press on society. Eisenstein examines various theories of the press and provides examples, some of which support while others unbalance the different theoretical approaches. An invaluable resource for writers of print media.

Marris, P. & Thornham, S. (Eds.). (2000). *Media studies: A reader* (2nd ed.). New York: New York University.

Covers the full range of media theories, from the Frankfurt School to American communication studies and the Canadian media theorists.

Critical European schools of thought are emphasized. A good introduction to the field of media studies.

Masterman, L. (1985). *Teaching the media*. London: Routledge.

Researchers will find this book useful for understanding the role of media in society. It also provides a review of media theory.

McLuhan, M. (1964). *Understanding media*. London: Routledge.

This classic text offers a comprehensive overview of media, especially electronic media, and their influence on human communication and society. Written almost half a century ago, this book raises questions that are still being discussed in media studies.

National Television Violence Study (3 vols.). (1996–1998). Thousand Oaks, CA: Sage.

The result of a cooperative effort of four universities, as well as a number of organizations, the examination of hours of television programs resulted in this three-volume analysis. This study offers a comprehensive report on violence on television (e.g., in the movies, children's programs, talk shows, etc.) with the focus on the effects it has on viewers, especially younger ones.

Tunstall, J. (2008). *The media were American: U.S. media in decline*. New York: Oxford.

In this follow-up to his 1977 *The media are American* (London: Constable), the author outlines how U.S. media industries have lost their position at the center of the media industry and must now compete in a world market.

Encyclopedias

Because they offer a quick review of the important information on a media topic, encyclopedias are very helpful to writers, especially at the initial stages of the research-and-writing process. A good encyclopedia presents clearly written, well-balanced coverage of a topic or issue and provides readers with a general introduction to a topic. Most encyclopedias provide a list of references and further readings that can help steer the reader toward more in-depth studies.

Blanchard, M. A. (Ed.). (1998). *History of the mass media in the United States: An encyclopedia*. Chicago: Fitzroy Dearborn Publishers.

Articles emphasize the development of news and information media in the United States, from the first newspaper in the American colonies in

1690 to the electronic media of the 1990s. Articles examine technological, legal, economic, and political developments that influenced the growth of the media. Entertainment media are covered, but to a lesser extent than news media. Some of the topical entries are advertising, alternative media, books, broadcasting, cable, design, legal issues, magazines, mass media, motion pictures, news agencies, photography, political figures in the media, public relations, radio, reporting, technology, television, and war. Most topics are followed by a list for further reading.

Hudson, R. V. (1987). *Mass media: A chronological encyclopedia of television, radio, motion pictures, magazines, newspapers and books in the United States*. New York: Garland Publishing, Inc.

Valuable source for checking facts, trends, and historic moments in U.S. mass media. Starts with the founding of the first press in the English Colonies in 1638 and ends with media developments in 1985. Emphasis is on achievements, dates, events, and people.

Johnson, D. H. (2003). *Encyclopedia of international media and communications* (Vols. 1–4). New York: Academic Press.

This four-volume set provides articles about the different media found around the world. It covers various types of media, such as books, magazines, film, computers, Internet, and phones; distribution systems, media institutions, media issues, and media concepts are also addressed. A good source for topics about international media.

Kaid, L. L. & Holtz–Bacha, C. (2008). *Encyclopedia of political communication*. Thousand Oaks, CA: Sage.

Almost 600 articles shed light on the role of media in the political process. While it provides an international perspective on the role of communication, including the mass media, in governance, its main focus is on U.S. politics and media. Topics include the role of newspapers in politics, blogs, blogging, and the Supreme Court and the media.

Murray, M. D. (Ed.). (1998). *Encyclopedia of television news*. Phoenix, AZ: Oryx Press.

Covers history, issues, and personalities related to television news. Readers will find information about ethical issues in TV news, the Federal Communication Commisssion, and the influence of the Internet on TV news. Information about many important TV news personalities is also included.

Newcomb, H. (2004). *Museum of broadcast communications: Encyclopedia of television* (2nd ed.) (Vols. 1—4). New York: Taylor & Francis.

This four-volume overview of the field of television contains well over 1,000 entries. It covers issues, people, and policies related to television. The articles are in-depth and fully cited. (Full disclosure: Raul Tovares contributed several articles to the *Encyclopedia of Television*). Online articles (first edition only) provide links to other encyclopedia entries related to the topic at hand. Available at: URL: http://www.museum.tv/publicationssection.php?page=520.

Schaefer, T. M. & Brickland, T. A. (Eds.). (2007). *Encyclopedia of media and politics*. Washington, DC: CQ Press.

One volume that covers the role of mass media in the production and transmission of information. Included are reviews of topics and brief profiles of persons who made significant contributions to the field of media and politics. The evolution of the media, their influence, the press and government institutions, and significant legal cases are only some of the issues covered. A list of references follows most of the articles.

Schement, J. R. (2002). *Encyclopedia of communication and information* (Vols. 1—3). New York: Macmillan Reference USA (an imprint of Gale Group).

This three-volume encyclopedia covers a broad spectrum of the field of communication. Eight general topics cover almost 300 topics: Careers, information science, information technologies, literacy, institutional studies, interpersonal communication, library science, and media effects. (Full disclosure: Alla Tovares (Yelyseieva) is a contributor to the *Encyclopedia of Communication and Information*).

Stavans, I. (2005). *Encyclopedia Latina: History, culture, and society* (Vols. 1—4). Danbury, Conn.: Grolier.

Includes many biographical entries about Latinos in media, from Hollywood stars to television personalities. Also includes entries on different Spanish-language media, such as television, radio, and newspapers. (Full disclosure: Raul Tovares contributed several articles to the *Encyclopedia Latina: History, culture, and society*).

Sterling, C. H. (2009). *Encyclopedia of journalism* (Vols. 1—6). Thousand Oaks, CA: Sage.

This six-volume encyclopedia gives its readers a wide-ranging view of the field of journalism. It analyzes the profession, business, and culture of journalism against national and international backdrops. An excellent source for starting research for a paper or report on an aspect of journalism: history, print, and electronic.

Sterling, C. H. & Keith, M. (Eds.). (2004). *Museum of broadcast communications: Encyclopedia of radio* (Vols. 1–3). New York: Taylor & Francis.

Three volumes provide an overview of radio broadcasting with an emphasis on the United States and other English-speaking countries, although other international entries are also included. African American, Hispanic, and Native American radio are also covered. An index helps locate smaller topics in longer articles; the bibliography, at the beginning of Volume 1 (p. xiii–xxvii), includes a listing of radio books, periodicals, and Internet Web sites. Because of the emphasis on broadcasting, topics such as telephone, data transmissions, and mobile phone transmissions are not included.

Research and Writing Texts

There are several good general or specialized writing and research textbooks available to media writers and researchers. Some of the most helpful include:

Booth, W. C., Colomb, G. G., & Williams, J. M. (2008). *The craft of research* (3rd ed.). Chicago & London: University of Chicago Press.

This book offers a comprehensive step-by-step guide for experienced and novice researchers on how to approach a research project. It addresses broad questions like what research is and how to formulate a good research question, along with an in-depth discussion of the logical structure of an argument. The Appendix lists bibliographic resources, with a separate section (pp. 298–299) dedicated to communication, journalism, and media studies.

George, M. W. (2008). *The elements of library research: What every student needs to know.* Princeton, NJ: Princeton University.

Easy-to-read introduction to library research. George provides helpful appendices. Appendix C is a timeline for writing and research; Appendix D consists of questions students should ask their instructors about the writing project; and Appendix E is a Research Appointment Worksheet to help students prepare for discussions about their research projects with their professors or a research librarian. The glossary and bibliography are also helpful.

Hacker, D. (2008). *A pocket style manual* (5th ed.). Boston, MA: Bedford/
    St. Martins.
A classic that writers, including media writers, will find useful. Most
first-year college students will already have a copy. The book's emphasis is
on writing, but one chapter covers research.

Kolln, M. & Funk, R. (2009). *Understanding English grammar* (8th ed.).
    New York: Pearson Education.
Instead of the usual "do's" and "don'ts" of grammar, this book provides a
thoughtful discussion of grammar. Sentence diagrams are used as illustrations.
Although not an easy text, this book will be appreciated by writers who strive
to understand patterns, principles, and the traditions of English grammar.

Lunsford, A. (2006). *Easy writer: A pocket reference* (3rd ed.). Boston: Bed-
    ford/St. Martins.
This writing reference starts with the 20 most common mistakes made
by students in their research papers. It also includes chapters that cover
grammar, sentence style, punctuation, and language. A chapter is also dedicated to common problems frequently experienced by international (multi-
lingual) students.

Palmquist, M. (2009). *The Bedford researcher* (3rd ed.). Boston, MA:
    Bedford/St. Martins.
From finding a topic to formatting a researcher paper, the book takes the
reader through the process of researching and writing a paper in the
humanities and social sciences. Much of the information applies to writing
media papers as well.

Rubin, R. B., Rubin, A. M., & Piele, L. J. (2005). *Communication research:
    Strategies and source* (6th ed.). Belmont, CA: Thomson/Wadsworth.
A thorough account of the research process in the field of communication.
Focus is on selecting, narrowing, and researching a topic. Information in the
chapters is followed by examples and exercises. The authors provide basics of
APA format (Appendix A) and useful glossary (Appendix B). Accompanying
Web site is accessible through: URL: http://communication.wadsworth.com.

Slade, C. & Perrin, R. (2008). *Form and style: Research papers, reports, theses*
    (13th ed.). Boston & New York: Houghton Mifflin Company.
Guides its readers through the process of research and writing, from
selecting a topic to formatting the final draft. Information about different
documentation styles (Chicago, MLA, APA) is also included. The glossary

provides meanings for the terms and abbreviations that often occur in academic and other formal writing.

Williams, J. (2007). *Style: Lessons in clarity and grace* (9th ed.). New York: Longman/Pearson.

Equips writers with helpful tools to construct effective sentences, cohesive paragraphs, and coherent texts. Each chapter contains tips, examples, exercises, and a helpful summary. The book also includes a review of punctuation (Appendix), a glossary, and suggested answers to exercises. A useful resource for those who want to write clearly, effectively, and gracefully.

ELECTRONIC RESOURCES
Online Writing Resources

Diana Hacker. "Research and Documentation Online." http://www.diana-hacker. com/resdoc/

Provides electronic sources in four areas: Humanities, Social Sciences, History, and Sciences. List of communication resources, including media resources, can be found in the Social Science tab. A sample paper is also available.

Purdue Online Writing Lab (OWL). http://owl.english.purdue.edu

This is an invaluable resource for students and professionals. The site has sections for ESL students, non-Purdue instructors and students, professional writers, and more. Under the heading of *Non—Purdue College Instructors and Students*, writers can find information ranging from how to get started writing a research paper to how to avoid writer's block, conduct research, avoid plagiarism, and cite properly. Definitely a site to be bookmarked.

Sage Publications: "Research and the Research Paper." http://infotrac. thomsonlearningcom/infowrite/research.html
http://infotrac.thomsonlearning.com/infowrite/index.html

An excellent site for a quick review of the basics of academic writing. The site covers (among other topics) the research paper, grammar, the writing process, and critical thinking. While not focused on media writing per se, its advice and ideas apply to media writing.

Online Research Databases

Google Scholar. http://scholar.google.com/

A useful site, especially at the beginning of a research project. It provides easy access to relevant cross-disciplinary scholarly publications: peer-reviewed articles, books, and abstracts. Writers can use Google Scholar to find articles ranging from a wide variety of academic publishers, professional societies, pre-print repositories, and universities, as well as scholarly articles available across the Web.

JSTOR. http://www.jstor.org/

Most university libraries subscribe to this database of full-text articles from academic journals in a number of disciplines, including arts, humanities, and social sciences. The articles can be read online or downloaded as PDF files.

EbscoHost (Academic Search Premier). http://web.ebscohost.com

Similar to JSTOR, this premium database is available through library subscription. It is updated daily and offers more than 4,000 full-text academic publications, primarily from peer-reviewed journals. It also provides electronic access to books and reference databases, and includes publications dating back to 1975.

Project Muse. http://muse.jhu.edu

Writers can access this database through a subscribing library. Publications can be searched either by the title of the journal, discipline, or by the subject heading of the article. Provides access to more than 400 titles from a number of the scholarly societies and university presses worldwide.

Online Media Research Resources

Berkman Center for Internet & Society. http://cyber.law.harvard.edu/

Publishes studies related to media and also keeps track of legal cases affecting freedom of the press and media access.

FactCheck. http://www.factcheck.org/about/

Associated with the Annenberg Public Policy Center, University of Pennsylvania. FactCheck assesses the accuracy of political statements made by politicians, political parties, and organizations in speeches, TV ads, political speeches, interviews, and press releases. List of sources accompanies analysis on FactCheck.

Miller Center of Public Affairs, University of Virginia. http://millercenter. org/scripps/archive/speeches

A good source for researchers interested in presidential inaugural speeches, as well as other important speeches delivered by U.S. presidents. All speeches are in transcript form, but some of the most recent are also in audio format. The Miller Center also maintains a Web site for its *Presidential Recordings Program*, which offers almost 5,000 hours of presidential meetings and telephone conversations recorded by six American presidents.

Museum of Broadcast Communications. http://www.museum.tv/

Has *Encyclopedia of Television, First Edition*, online. Also provides video of classic commercials and online civil rights collection.

Pew Research Center for the People & the Press http://people-press.org/
reports/

The Center for the People & the Press is a nonpartisan organization that conducts surveys to measure attitudes about a variety of issues. In its News Interest Index, a weekly survey, the Center reports on the events people are interested in and their opinions about those events. Recent surveys give an account of the public's views of science, and scientists' views of how the media cover science.

Poynter Institute. http://www.poynter.org/

The Poynter Institute is designed to provide educational excellence to journalists, future journalists, and those who teach journalism. Its Web site contains valuable discussions on current issues in journalism, and Poynter bibliographies that provide links to a number of online media resources and organizations: http://www.poynter.org/content/content_view.asp?id=896.

Online Communication Studies Resources

University of Iowa, College of Liberal Arts & Sciences, Department of Communication Studies. http://www.uiowa.edu/commstud/resources/index.html

An excellent online source for news and information about media matters, as well as tools such as LISTSERVs, journals, citation guides, and much more. Worth taking a look.

Professional Organizations

Association for Education in Journalism & Mass Communication (AEJMC). http://www.aejmc.org/

Web site offers abstracts of papers presented at its national conventions going back to 1997. Copies of papers presented at conventions are also available for a fee. Paper topics are related to Divisions and Interest Groups withing the organization.

National Communication Association (NCA). http://www.natcom.org/index.asp?sid=34

NCA's Communication Currents site (http://www.communication currents.com/) is a source for ideas for research paper topics. Essays in Communication Currents, an online Web magazine, are selected from NCA journals.

INDEX

About the Authors

RAÚL DAMACIO TOVARES is associate professor in the communication program at Trinity Washington University, Washington, DC. In 2002 Dr. Tovares' *Manufacturing the Gang: Mexican American Youth on Local Television News*, was published by Greenwood. Dr. Tovares' articles have appeared in the *Journal of Broadcast Education*, the *Howard Journal of Communications*, and the *Journal of Communication Inquiry*. He has also contributed to the *Encyclopedia of Television* and the *Encyclopedia Latina*. Several of his essays have appeared as chapters in books. Dr. Tovares is a member of the *National Communication Association* (NCA) and the *Association for Educators in Journalism and Mass Communication* (AEJMC). His major areas of interest are media theory, news production, minorities and mass communication, intercultural communication, and film theory.

ALLA V. TOVARES is assistant professor in the department of English at Howard University. Her research interests include public/private intertextuality in media and everyday discourse, family discourse, dialogicality in literary discourse and everyday conversations. Her articles have appeared in *Text and Talk* and the *Encyclopedia of Communication and Information*. She contributed a chapter to *Family Talk: Discourse and Identity in Four American Families*, Oxford University press. Dr. Tovares is a member of the *American Association for Applied Linguistics* and *International Pragmatics Association*. She is currently interested in the internal polemic of endurance athletes' self-talk and the life and work of African American Shakespearian actor Ira Aldridge (1807–1867).